DATE DUE

Demco, Inc. 38-293

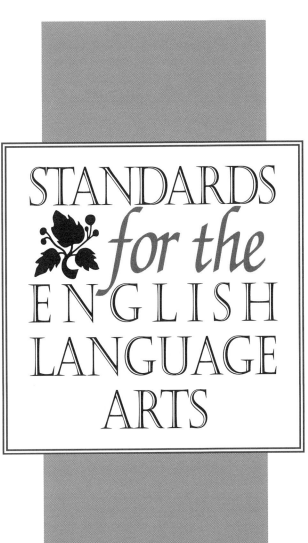

NATIONAL COUNCIL OF TEACHERS OF ENGLISH
1111 W. Kenyon Road, Urbana, Illinois 61801-1096

INTERNATIONAL READING ASSOCIATION
800 Barksdale Road, P.O. Box 8139, Newark, Delaware 19714-8139

Cover design: Boni Nash, IRA Graphic Design Coordinator
Interior design: Larry Husfelt, IRA Design Consultant
Manuscript editors: Michael Greer, Rona S. Smith, Lee Erwin, NCTE

IRA Stock Number: 889
NCTE Stock Number: 46767-3050

Photo Credits: Bill Leece (p. 4); Thompson-McClellan Photography (pp. 6, 9, 11, 18, 22, 29, 32, 35, 39, 43, 44); Ray Martens (pp. 15, 54); Susan Lina Ruggles (pp. 50, 57, 58, 59, 62); George Rattin and Mike Jankowski (p. 64).

High School Vignette 4 is adapted from *The Writer's Craft, Orange Level;* copyright ©1992 by McDougal, Littell & Company, Box 1667, Evanston, IL 60204. All rights reserved.

The Korean text appearing in Middle School Vignette 3 is excerpted with permission from *Classroom Publishing: A Practical Guide to Enhancing Student Literacy,* published by Blue Heron Publishing, Hillsboro, Oregon.

Library of Congress Cataloging-in-Publication Data
National Council of Teachers of English.
    Standards for the English language arts.
      p. cm.
    Includes bibliographical references.
    ISBN 0-8141-4676-7 (pbk.)
      1. Language arts—United States—Standards. I. International
Reading Association. II. Title.
LB1576.N274 1996
808'.042'071—dc20

96-3238
CIP

CONTENTS

Introduction	**vii**
Chapter 1: Setting Standards in the English Language Arts	**1**
Defining the Standards	1
The Need for Standards	2
To Prepare Students for the Literacy Demands of Today and Tomorrow	4
To Present a Shared Vision of Literacy Education	6
To Promote Equity and Excellence for All	8
Learning How to Learn	9
Equal Access to Resources	10
Adequate Staffing	10
Safe, Well-Equipped Schools	10
Chapter 2: Perspectives Informing the English Language Arts Standards	**12**
Literacy and Language Learning: An Interactive Model	12
Content	14
A Broad Range of Texts	15
Processes and Strategies	16
Systems and Structures of Language	16
Purpose	16
For Obtaining and Communicating Information	17
For Literary Response and Expression	17
For Learning and Reflection	17
For Problem Solving and Application	18
Development	18
How Students Acquire Knowledge and Develop Competency over Time	19

How Students Should Be Able to Use Language   20
   Clearly   20
   Strategically   20
   Critically   21
   Creatively   21
Context   21

Chapter 3: The English Language Arts Standards   24

IRA/NCTE Standards for the English Language Arts   25
The Standards in Detail   27
   Standard 1   27
   Standard 2   29
   Standard 3   31
   Standard 4   33
   Standard 5   35
   Standard 6   36
   Standard 7   38
   Standard 8   39
   Standard 9   41
   Standard 10   42
   Standard 11   44
   Standard 12   45
Realizing the Standards   46

Chapter 4: Standards in the Classroom   47

Elementary Vignettes   48
Middle School Vignettes   55
High School Vignettes   61

In Conclusion   68

Glossary   70

Appendix A: List of Participants   78

Appendix B: History of the Standards Project   110

Appendix C: Overview of Standards Projects   112

Appendix D: State and International English Language Arts Standards   114

Appendix E: Resources for Teachers   119

Appendix F: Response to *Standards for the English Language Arts*   132

INTRODUCTION

The International Reading Association and the National Council of Teachers of English are pleased to present these standards for the English language arts. This document is the result of an intensive four-year project involving thousands of educators, researchers, parents, policymakers, and others across the country. Our shared purpose is to ensure that all students are knowledgeable and proficient users of language so that they may succeed in school, participate in our democracy as informed citizens, find challenging and rewarding work, appreciate and contribute to our culture, and pursue their own goals and interests as independent learners throughout their lives.

The English Language Arts Standards Project is one of many efforts undertaken in recent years to define outcomes or goals for various school subjects. The project was first proposed in an August 1991 letter to U.S. Secretary of Education Lamar Alexander from Judith Thelen, then president of the International Reading Association (IRA), and Shirley Haley-James, then president of the National Council of Teachers of English (NCTE). If the federal government were to fund a voluntary standards project in English, then IRA and NCTE wanted to be involved. Our officers and committees believed—and still believe—that English language arts standards must be grounded in what we know about language and language learning. If the standards do not have this very important foundation, then they could undermine our nation's commitment to educating all students, to emerging conceptions of literacy, and to publicly funded schools. The standards presented here grew out of current research and theory about how students learn—in particular, how they learn language.

In the fall of 1992, the U.S. Department of Education awarded a grant for the Standards Project for the English Language Arts to educators at the Center for the Study of Reading at the University of Illinois with the agreement that the Center would work closely with IRA and NCTE to develop the standards. Federal involvement ended in 1994, and from that time until the present the project has been funded solely by IRA and NCTE.

Two principles endorsed by the National Academy of Education (McLaughlin and Shepard 1995, p. xviii) have been central to our work:

■ Because there is not one best way to organize subject matter in a given field of study, rigorous national standards should not be restricted to one set of standards per subject area.

- Content standards should embody a coherent, professionally defensible conception of how a field can be framed for purposes of instruction. They should not be an exhaustive, incoherent compendium of every group's desired content.

From its inception, the English Language Arts Standards Project has been field-based. A guiding belief has been that the process of defining standards must be an open, inclusive one. As a result, thousands of K–12 classroom teachers have been involved in writing, reviewing, and revising the many successive drafts of this document and have guided its development every step of the way over the last three-and-a-half years. Hundreds of parents, legislative leaders, administrators, researchers, and policy analysts in English language arts have played critical roles at each stage of the project. (Appendix A lists participants in the process.)

In generating this document, we have sought to reflect the many different voices, interests, and concerns of these diverse contributors. While we recognize that no single publication, no single set of standards, can satisfy all interests and concerns, we fervently hope that this work captures the essential goals of English language arts instruction at the turn of the century in the United States of America. Most important, we hope that it offers a coherent vision for the future, complementing other current efforts to define performance standards, opportunity-to-learn standards, and assessment standards not only in the English language arts but in other school subject areas as well. Many states and local districts are already using these standards in their deliberations, and we have benefited from the responses of language arts coordinators in every state.

The publication of this document represents not only the end of one process, that of defining the standards, but also the beginning of a new one—that of translating them into practice in classrooms across the country. The conversation about English language arts standards must and will continue. To that end, we are enclosing a response form at the end of this document. We invite you—in fact, we urge you—to tell us what you think about our vision of the English language arts curriculum.

We extend our deepest thanks to the thousands of individuals who have participated in the standards project to date. Thank you for contributing your voices to this important national conversation. We also wish to thank the College Board and the John D. and Catherine T. MacArthur Foundation for their funding of the project at the beginning of the journey.

Alan E. Farstrup
International Reading Association

Miles Myers
National Council of Teachers of English

REFERENCE
McLaughlin, M. W., & Shepard, L. A., with O'Day, J. A. (1995). *Improving education through standards-based reform: A report by the National Academy of Education Panel on Standards-Based Education Reform.* Stanford, CA: National Academy of Education.

CHAPTER 1

SETTING STANDARDS IN THE ENGLISH LANGUAGE ARTS

This document describes standards for the English language arts—that is, it defines what students should know about language and be able to do with language. Our goal is to define, as clearly and specifically as possible, the current consensus among literacy teachers and researchers about what students should learn in the English language arts—reading, writing, listening, speaking, viewing, and visually representing. The ultimate purpose of these standards is to ensure that *all* students are offered the opportunities, the encouragement, and the vision to develop the language skills they need to pursue life's goals, including personal enrichment and participation as informed members of our society.

Over the past several years, national educational organizations have launched a series of ambitious projects to define voluntary standards for science, mathematics, art, music, foreign languages, social studies, English language arts, and other subjects. These efforts have served as catalysts in a wide-ranging national conversation about the needs of students and the instructional approaches of their teachers. This dialogue is healthy and speaks well of the value placed on education by the American public.

This document adds to the national dialogue by presenting the consensus that exists among thousands of English language arts educators about what all students in K–12 schools should know and be able to do with language, in all its forms. We believe that the act of defining standards is worthwhile because it invites further reflection and conversation about the fundamental goals of public schooling.

DEFINING THE STANDARDS

Based on extensive discussions among educators across the country about the central aims of English language arts instruction, the International Reading Association and the National Council of Teachers of English have defined a set of content standards for the English language arts. By the term *content standards*, we mean statements that define what students should know and be able to do in the English language arts. Although the standards focus primarily on content, we also underscore the importance of other dimensions of language learning. In particular, we believe that questions of why, when, and how students grow and develop as language users are also critical and must be addressed by those who translate the standards into practice. As we discuss in Chapter 2, the perspective informing the standards captures the interaction among these aspects of language learning—content, purpose, development, and context—and emphasizes the central role of the learner, whose goals and interests drive the processes of learning.

In defining the standards, we use some terms that have multiple meanings. Briefly, we use the term *text* broadly to refer not only to printed texts, but also to spoken language, graphics, and technological communications. *Language* as it is used here encompasses visual communication in addition to spoken and written forms of expression. And *reading* refers to listening and viewing in addition to print-oriented reading. (See the Glossary for additional terms.)

It is important to emphasize from the outset that these standards are intended to serve as guidelines that provide ample room for the kinds of innovation and creativity that are essential to teaching and learning. They are not meant to be seen as prescriptions for particular curricula or instructional approaches.

We must also stress that although a list implies that the individual entries are distinct and clearly separable, the realities of language learning are far more complex. Each of these standards is tied to the others in obvious and subtle ways, and considerable overlap exists among them. Thus, while we identify discrete standards for purposes of discussion and elaboration, and to provide a curricular focus, we recognize the complex interactions that exist among the individual entries and urge our readers to do the same.

Subsequent chapters of this document explore a model of language learning that provides a perspective for standards (Chapter 2); elaborate on the standards (Chapter 3); and consider some of the ways in which the standards are realized in the classroom (Chapter 4). Before turning to these discussions, however, we wish to take a closer look at the rationale for setting standards—why we believe defining standards is important and what we hope to accomplish in doing so.

While we identify discrete standards for purposes of discussion and elaboration, and to provide a curricular focus, we recognize the complex interactions that exist among the individual entries and urge our readers to do the same.

THE NEED FOR STANDARDS

In defining standards for the English language arts, we are motivated by three core beliefs:

- First, we believe that standards are needed to prepare students for the literacy requirements of the future as well as the present. Changes in

IRA/NCTE
STANDARDS FOR THE ENGLISH LANGUAGE ARTS

❧

The vision guiding these standards is that all students must have the opportunities and resources to develop the language skills they need to pursue life's goals and to participate fully as informed, productive members of society. These standards assume that literacy growth begins before children enter school as they experience and experiment with literacy activities—reading and writing, and associating spoken words with their graphic representations. Recognizing this fact, these standards encourage the development of curriculum and instruction that make productive use of the emerging literacy abilities that children bring to school. Furthermore, the standards provide ample room for the innovation and creativity essential to teaching and learning. They are not prescriptions for particular curriculum or instruction.

Although we present these standards as a list, we want to emphasize that they are not distinct and separable; they are, in fact, interrelated and should be considered as a whole.

1. Students read a wide range of print and nonprint texts to build an understanding of texts, of themselves, and of the cultures of the United States and the world; to acquire new information; to respond to the needs and demands of society and the workplace; and for personal fulfillment. Among these texts are fiction and nonfiction, classic and contemporary works.

2. Students read a wide range of literature from many periods in many genres to build an understanding of the many dimensions (e.g., philosophical, ethical, aesthetic) of human experience.

3. Students apply a wide range of strategies to comprehend, interpret, evaluate, and appreciate texts. They draw on their prior experience, their interactions with other readers and writers, their knowledge of word meaning and of other texts, their word identification strategies, and their understanding of textual features (e.g., sound-letter correspondence, sentence structure, context, graphics).

4. Students adjust their use of spoken, written, and visual language (e.g., conventions, style, vocabulary) to communicate effectively with a variety of audiences and for different purposes.

5. Students employ a wide range of strategies as they write and use different writing process elements appropriately to communicate with different audiences for a variety of purposes.

6. Students apply knowledge of language structure, language conventions (e.g., spelling and punctuation), media techniques, figurative language, and genre to create, critique, and discuss print and nonprint texts.

7. Students conduct research on issues and interests by generating ideas and questions, and by posing problems. They gather, evaluate, and synthesize data from a variety of sources (e.g., print and nonprint texts, artifacts, people) to communicate their discoveries in ways that suit their purpose and audience.

8. Students use a variety of technological and informational resources (e.g., libraries, databases, computer networks, video) to gather and synthesize information and to create and communicate knowledge.

9. Students develop an understanding of and respect for diversity in language use, patterns, and dialects across cultures, ethnic groups, geographic regions, and social roles.

10. Students whose first language is not English make use of their first language to develop competency in the English language arts and to develop understanding of content across the curriculum.

11. Students participate as knowledgeable, reflective, creative, and critical members of a variety of literacy communities.

12. Students use spoken, written, and visual language to accomplish their own purposes (e.g., for learning, enjoyment, persuasion, and the exchange of information).

technology and society have altered and will continue to alter the ways in which we use language to communicate and to think. Students must be prepared to meet these demands.

- Second, we believe that standards can articulate a shared vision of what the nation's teachers, literacy researchers, teacher educators, parents, and others expect students to attain in the English language arts, and what we can do to ensure that this vision is realized.

- Third, we believe that standards are necessary to promote high educational expectations for all students and to bridge the documented disparities that exist in educational opportunities. Standards can help us ensure that all students become informed citizens and participate fully in society.

To Prepare Students for the Literacy Demands of Today and Tomorrow

The standards outlined in this document reflect a view of literacy that is both broader and more demanding than traditional definitions. For many years, literacy was defined in a very limited way—as the ability to read or write one's own name, for example (Soltow and Stevens 1981). A much more ambitious definition of literacy today includes the capacity to accomplish a wide range of reading, writing, and other language tasks associated with everyday life. The National Literacy Act of 1991, for example, defines literacy as "an individual's ability to read, write, and speak in English and compute and solve problems at levels of proficiency necessary to function on the job and in society, to achieve one's goals, and to develop one's knowledge and potential."

This historical perspective provides a context for interpreting current perspectives on English language arts education. For example, critics argue that fewer and fewer students are able to read and write well, blaming schools

and teachers for failing to fulfill their responsibilities. In actuality, however, ever-increasing numbers of high school graduates have met our past goals in literacy (see sidebar). The mismatch that currently exists is between students' achievements and our expanded expectation for their literacy.

We see the need for change, but this need derives from a vision of a more challenging future rather than a criticism of past or current efforts. We believe that schools and teachers deserve praise for the encouraging results they are achieving. This does not mean, however, that all students today leave school with every skill they need to become critically literate citizens, workers, members of soci-

Standards for the English Language Arts

ety, and lifelong learners. Indeed, we face new demands, new standards of critical thinking and expressive ability, that we are now beginning to meet.

Literacy expectations are likely to accelerate in the coming decades. To participate fully in society and the workplace in 2020, citizens will need powerful literacy abilities that until now have been achieved by only a small percentage of the population. At the same time, individuals will need to develop technological competencies undreamed of as recently as ten years ago. One unexpected outcome of the recent explosion in electronic media has been a remarkable increase in the use of written language, suggesting that predictions about the decline of conventional literacy have been misplaced and premature. Electronic mail, similarly, has fundamentally altered personal written correspondence, and growing access to the Internet will continue to increase the demand for citizens who can read and write using electronic media. Furthermore, reading and writing are essential skills in planning and producing nonprint media.

This broadened definition of literacy means that English language arts education must address many different types and uses of language, including those that are often given limited attention in the curriculum. One such area is spoken language. We have learned to respect the continuing importance of oral culture in all communities and to recognize the rich interdependence between spoken and written language. Much of our knowledge of language and our acquisition of literacy depends on spoken language. Any definition of the English language arts must therefore include helping students learn how to accomplish successfully the many functions of spoken language, such as discussing texts, making presentations, assisting visitors, or telling stories to family and friends.

Being literate in contemporary society means being active, critical, and creative users not only of print and spoken language but also of the visual language of film and television, commercial and political advertising, photography, and more. Teaching students how to interpret and create visual texts such as illustrations, charts, graphs, electronic

Three sources of data indicate that, contrary to popular belief, reading and writing abilities have not declined over time: "then and now" studies, test restandardization research, and the National Assessment of Educational Progress surveys of reading and writing.

By readministering the same test over time, "then and now" studies examine trends in student achievement based on past standards of literacy. Of the several dozen studies of this nature, all but one conclude that more recent students outperform earlier students (Farr, Tuinman, and Rowls 1974). The exception was found in a study comparing the skills of pre-1930 students and post-1935 students in oral reading, an area that was de-emphasized in the reading curriculum in the early 1930s.

When test publishers revise (or "restandardize") an aging test, they administer both old and new versions to a sample of current students. A review of test restandardization reports indicates that, since the mid-1970s, scores have increased by about 2 percentile points per year for five of the six most widely used achievement tests in grades 1 through 9. Changes in scores at the high school level have been mixed, with scores increasing slightly on some tests and decreasing slightly on others (Berliner and Biddle 1995; Linn, Graue, and Sanders 1990; Kibby 1993, 1995; Stedman and Kaestle 1987).

The National Assessment of Educational Progress (NAEP) conducts periodic assessments of reading, writing, and other subject areas with nationally representative samples of 9-, 13-, and 17-year-olds. Since 1971, there has been a statistically significant increase in reading scores among 13- and 17-year-olds (Mullis, Campbell, and Farstrup 1993).

Thus, evidence suggests that students today read better and write better than at any other time in the history of the country (Kibby 1993, 1995).

displays, photographs, film, and video is another essential component of the English language arts curriculum. Visual communication is part of the fabric of contemporary life. Although many parents and teachers worry that television, film, and video have displaced reading and encouraged students to be passive, unreflective, and uninvolved, we cannot erase visual texts from modern life even if we want to. We must therefore challenge students to analyze critically the texts they view and to integrate their visual knowledge with their knowledge of other forms of language. By studying how visual texts work, students learn to employ visual media as another powerful means of communication.

Based on this expanded definition of literacy, the standards outlined in this document address six English language arts: reading, writing, speaking, listening, viewing, and visually representing. These six areas are notably different from one another, but there are also important connections among them, and these connections are central to English language arts instruction and learning. One familiar way to link the language arts, for example, is to pair them by medium: reading and writing involve written language, listening and speaking involve spoken communication, and viewing and visually representing involve visual language.

There are many other important interconnections among the English language arts, as well. Learners' repertoires of words, images, and concepts grow as they read, listen, and view; new words, images, and concepts then become part of their written, spoken, and visual language systems. We know, for example, that in the early stages of reading, the act of writing helps to shape children's understanding of texts. Children use a number of strategies for writing. Sometimes they read the stories they have composed to classmates to get feedback on what is working well in their stories and what needs clarifying. Sometimes they spell a word the way it sounds (that is, applying their knowledge of phonics), while at other times they spell a word the way they recall seeing it. These writing/spelling strategies draw children's attention to the conventions of print, enabling them to begin to read like writers.

Thus, English language arts learning activities are seldom wholly discrete—"just reading," "just writing," or "just viewing," for example. Each medium relates directly or indirectly to every other.

To Present a Shared Vision of Literacy Education

Clearly defined standards offer a vision of the knowledge and strategies that all students should develop in the English language arts, as well as of the curricular and instructional elements that can be used to foster this development. To achieve these standards, this vision must be shared by all those who have a stake in the future of our schools—not just the English language arts teachers who are directly responsible for providing instruction, but also school administrators, policymakers, parents, and members of the general public. A shared vision means that different parties know what the work of the classroom is and should be, and have a clear sense of what they can do to support this work. Public commitments to education may depend upon this shared vision.

A shared vision does not, of course, imply a single approach to teaching. Teachers know that their students develop language competencies in different ways and at different rates, and that learning needs must be addressed as they arise and in the ways that seem most appropriate. Adaptability and creativity are far more effective in the classroom than thoroughgoing applications of a single approach. Most teachers' experience validates this philosophy every day. They recognize that no single instructional method or sequence of lessons can serve all students or all situations.

Despite the array of instructional approaches being used in individual classrooms, teachers do appear to share many views about teaching and learning in the English language arts. What are these views? What are some of the elements of this common vision?

First, and most important, teachers share a belief that students should develop competencies in the English language arts that will prepare them for the diverse literacy demands that will face them throughout their lives. Second, teachers agree that the English language arts are important not only as subjects in and of themselves, but also as supporting skills for students' learning in all other subjects. The English language arts help students gather and convey information about mathematics, history, science, the arts, and an array of other subjects, and in all of these subjects students use language to solve problems, theorize, and synthesize. Third, teachers agree that students can best develop language competencies (like other competencies) through meaningful activities and settings, such as reading and viewing whole texts, writing and creating visual images for recognizable purposes, and speaking and listening to others both within and outside the classroom.

Obviously, however, it is not enough simply to set forth a shared vision: English language arts teachers must also identify and remove the barriers that prevent that vision from being translated into practice. For example, teachers often receive conflicting messages about what they should be doing. They may be told they should respond to the need for reforms and innovations while at the same time being discouraged from making their instructional practices look too different from those of the past.

In addition, while many teachers wish to gauge their students' learning using performance-based assessment, they find that preparing students for machine-scored tests—which often focus on isolated skills rather than contextualized learning—diverts valuable classroom time away from the development of actual performance. Similarly, in many schools, the pressure to use particular textbooks discourages teachers from using materials that take advantage of students' interests and needs and that involve them productively in the curriculum. In these schools, students may be forced to follow prescribed sequences of instruction rather than engage in authentic, open-ended learning experiences. So, too, the widespread practice of dividing the class day into separate periods precludes integration among the English language arts and other subject areas.

Thus, while the shared vision of English language arts education we describe is already being implemented in many classrooms, there is clearly a need to do more. By articulating standards, we hope to make it easier for a shared vision to become a reality.

To Promote Equity and Excellence for All

One of our nation's greatest aspirations has been to provide equal educational opportunities for all. It is clear, however, that we have frequently fallen short of this goal with children of the poor, students from certain linguistic and cultural groups, and those in need of special education.

We believe that defining standards furnishes the occasion for examining the education of students who previously have not fully enjoyed prospects for high attainment. In a democracy, free and universal schooling is meant to prepare *all* students to become literate adults capable of critical thinking, listening, and reading, and skilled in speaking and writing. Failure to prepare our students for these tasks undermines not only our nation's vision of public education, but our democratic ideal. The consent of the governed is the basis of governmental legitimacy, and if that consent is not informed, then the foundations of government are shaky indeed.

Some of the most generously supported schools in the world are found in our nation's affluent suburbs, while many economically disadvantaged schools around the country are struggling to survive. A vast gulf in academic resources and accomplishments exists between the children of the rich and the children of the poor, and between the powerful and the powerless. This often leads to sharp differences in the opportunities provided to students with linguistic and cultural backgrounds that differ from those of mainstream students.

Students in special education programs in our country also often receive fewer educational opportunities than other students. Students designated as having learning disabilities, hearing or visual impairments, emotional or behavioral disorders, or who have orthopedic or cognitive disabilities do present us with instructional challenges. However, when we view these exceptional conditions as individual variations and provide personalized, expert instruction, students with disabilities can reach their academic potential.

It is, in fact, teachers' responsibility to recognize and value all children's rich and varied potentials for learning and to provide appropriate educational opportunities to nurture them. If we learn to recognize and value a variety of student abilities in the language arts and then build on those strengths, we make it possible for all students to attain high standards. Some will do so quickly and others more slowly, but to bridge the wide disparities in literacy attainment and to prepare all students to become informed and literate citizens, we must hold these high expectations for every student and every school. It is the responsibility not only of schools

While the shared vision of English language arts education we describe is already being implemented in many classrooms, there is clearly a need to do more.

Standards for the English Language Arts

and teachers, but also of policymakers, parents, and communities, to support the schools.

At the same time, we understand that standards, by themselves, cannot erase the impact of poverty, ethnic and cultural discrimination, family illiteracy, and social and political disenfranchisement. If all students are to receive equal educational opportunities and meet high expectations for performance, then these issues have to be addressed. Four factors are especially important: (a) learning how to learn, (b) equal access to school resources, (c) an adequate number of knowledgeable teachers, and (d) safe, well-equipped schools.

Learning How to Learn

Students not only need to develop specific competencies and to acquire knowledge—they also need abundant opportunities to reflect on the process of learning itself. The conscious process of learning how to learn is an essential element in students' language arts education, and it forms a central theme in the standards detailed in Chapter 3.

Knowing how to learn has not often been highlighted explicitly as part of instructional content in the English language arts. It has commonly been assumed that "bright" learners come by such knowledge "naturally" in the course of learning subject-matter content. The view of language learning presented here, in contrast, emphasizes the importance of explicit attention to the learning process for all students: learning how to learn ought to be considered as fundamental as other, more widely recognized, basic skills in English language arts.

All students have the ability to learn, but teachers can make that ability accessible by helping students reflect upon, and monitor, their own learning. When students see themselves as able learners, capable of monitoring and controlling their learning, they are more willing to tackle challenging tasks and take the risks that move their learning forward. As students move from school into their adult responsibilities at work and in the wider society, knowing how to learn will help them succeed in a changing economy and will enable them to become self-motivated, flexible lifelong learners.

By being attentive to, and talking about, their own learning strategies, students develop this sense of themselves as resourceful learners and provide their teachers with valuable insights into their development. If students are conscious of the strategies they use, they are better able to recognize when a familiar strategy is not working, and they are more prepared to adapt or abandon one strategy in favor of more effective alternatives.

Our conviction that all students can learn and can understand the processes of learning leads us to stress that all students can, with appropriate instruction and experiences, achieve high standards. The learner-centered perspective presented in this document is, therefore, also a learning-centered model. Teachers who implement this model help students see themselves as competent learners who understand the value of consciously reflecting upon their learning processes. Learning how to learn is at the heart of all of the standards and is reflected in various ways in each of them.

Equal Access to Resources

If all students are to have equal opportunities to meet these standards, then all schools must have sufficient funds to hire well-qualified teachers and staff, to acquire high-quality instructional materials, and to purchase essential supplies such as books, paper, and desks. This means that states and communities must address the often serious funding inequities across school districts. In most states, the wealthiest school districts spend two to five times as much per student as the poorest districts, and more than twenty years of community efforts and litigation have not resolved these structural inequalities. Today, as we write this document, there are public school teachers across the country who must spend their own money for their students to have even the minimum—pencils, paper, and books—in an era when computer technology is rapidly becoming a necessary part of instruction.

To be sure, money alone does not guarantee academic excellence. If funding is not used for constructive purposes such as obtaining better instructional materials, reducing class size, or supporting professional development, then all the money in the world will not improve student outcomes. Schools can be expected to help their students meet high standards, however, only if they possess adequate resources.

Adequate Staffing

Schools must also have an adequate number of knowledgeable teachers. Overcrowded classrooms make it virtually impossible to carry out the kinds of individualized and performance-oriented instruction essential to meeting the standards. Yet, in many schools, teachers are typically assigned to classrooms with thirty or forty students or more. In such settings, chances for meaningful interaction between teacher and student are slim, and opportunities for good teaching and learning are severely compromised.

It is not enough to have a sufficient number of well-qualified teachers, though; these teachers need to have access to ongoing opportunities for professional development. School districts need to provide both funding and support for teachers' attendance at off-site conferences and staff development programs. Teachers need opportunities to share ideas, engage in research, assist one another, and continue learning about and responding to changes in their fields. Schools need to nurture an atmosphere of learning that promotes teachers' growth along with that of their students.

Safe, Well-Equipped Schools

The current epidemic of violence in our schools and neighborhoods presents perhaps the single most serious threat to students' learning and to achieving the standards set forth here. Students deserve safe environments for learning. They can scarcely be expected to care about literacy or learning if they must constantly worry about being attacked in the hall or the schoolyard. Therefore, states and communities must do all they can to ensure that students are protected. Ideally, schools will become nurturing spaces where students are free to learn without the need for protection.

The condition and appearance of the school are also important aspects of the learning environment. Too many schools, particularly those in eco-

Only by being true to the full growth of all the individuals who make it up, can society . . . be true to itself.
—John Dewey,
School and Society

nomically disadvantaged communities, have suffered from years of neglect and are sadly in need of repair. Some schools recruit student volunteers and employees to help with painting and renovation, but in many cases the major repairs needed go well beyond the capabilities of volunteer workers. Communities should provide necessary resources to ensure that their schools are well-maintained, brightly lit, attractive settings that encourage learning.

In summary, IRA and NCTE hope and believe that the standards put forth in this document will prepare students for the literacy challenges they will face throughout their lives; bring greater coherence and clarity to teaching and learning in the English language arts; and provide greater opportunities for all students to become literate.

REFERENCES

Berliner, D. C., & Biddle, B. J. (1995). *The manufactured crisis: Exploding the myths and confronting the real problems of education.* Reading, MA: Addison-Wesley.

Farr, R., Tuinman, J., & Rowls, M. (1974). *Reading achievement in the United States.* Bloomington, IN: The Reading Program Center & the Institute for Child Study.

Kibby, M. W. (1993). What reading teachers should know about reading proficiency in the U.S. *Journal of Reading, 37,* 28–40.

Kibby, M. W. (1995). *Student literacy: Myths and realities (Fastback 381).* Bloomington, IN: Phi Delta Kappa Educational Foundation.

Linn, R. L., Graue, M. E., & Sanders, N. M. (1990). Comparing state and district test results to national norms: The validity of claims that "everyone is above average." *Educational Measurement: Issues and Practice, 9* (3), 5–14.

Mullis, I. V. S., Campbell, J. R., & Farstrup, A. E. (1993). *Executive summary of the NAEP 1992 reading report card for the nation and the states: Data from the national and trial state assessments.* Washington, DC: National Center for Educational Statistics.

Soltow, L., & Stevens, E. (1981). *The rise of literacy and the common school in the United States: A socioeconomic analysis to 1870.* Chicago: University of Chicago Press.

Stedman, L. C., & Kaestle, C. F. (1987). Literacy and reading performance in the United States, from 1800 to the present. *Reading Research Quarterly, 22,* 8–46.

CHAPTER 2

PERSPECTIVES INFORMING THE ENGLISH LANGUAGE ARTS STANDARDS

Language is the most powerful, most readily available tool we have for representing the world to ourselves and ourselves to the world. Language is not only a means of communication, it is a primary instrument of thought, a defining feature of culture, and an unmistakable mark of personal identity. Encouraging and enabling students to learn to use language effectively is certainly one of society's most important tasks.

Clearly, though, learning does not end the moment we graduate from school; it continues throughout our lives. In fact, the remarkable process of language learning keeps blossoming with each new experience we have—each book we read, each letter we write, each film we see, each message we hear. The aim of the standards, then, is to develop students' knowledge of, facility in, and appreciation of the English language in ways that will serve them throughout their lives.

This chapter presents the perspective that informs the standards, which are then defined in the next chapter. Specifically, we discuss the central role of the learner in the standards and explore four dimensions of literacy and language learning: content, purpose, development, and context. These dimensions provide distinct lenses through which one can examine the use of language and the learning of language use, all leading to the attainment of the standards.

LITERACY AND LANGUAGE LEARNING: AN INTERACTIVE MODEL

The perspective that informs the English language arts standards, presented graphically in Figure 1, places the learner at the core. The centrality of the learner is significant: our goal is to ground the standards in the experiences and activities of students as they read, write, speak, listen, view, and visually represent. Because the standards are learner-centered, they focus on the ways in which students participate in their own learning, acquire knowledge, shape experience, and respond to their own particular needs and goals through the English language arts. This reflects an active rather than a passive process of language use and learning—a process in which students' engagement is primary.

The three circles shown in the graphic represent the areas of primary emphasis and concern in language learning: content, purpose, and development. These three are not so much discrete entities as they are aspects or dimensions of learning. Briefly, the content dimension elaborates what students should learn in the English language arts; the purpose dimension articulates why students use the language arts; and the development dimension focuses on how students grow as language users. Surrounding these parts of the model is a field we have labeled "context." Because all language learning takes place in, responds to, shapes, and is in turn shaped by particular social and cultural contexts, this dimension encompasses the standards as a whole.

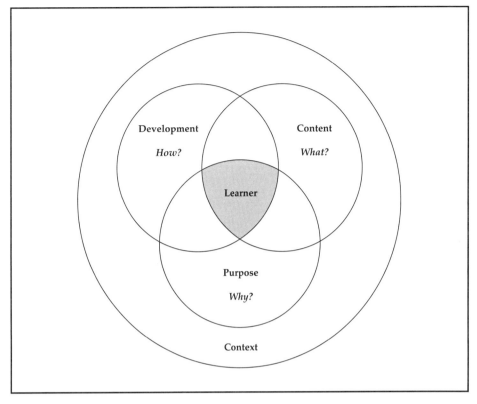

Figure 1. An Interactive Model for the English Language Arts Standards.

What precisely do we mean by these terms? Let us examine each dimension in turn.

The *content* dimension addresses what students should know and be able to do with the English language arts. This includes knowledge of written, spoken, and visual texts and of the processes involved in creating, interpreting, and critiquing such texts. Depending on the nature of the literacy task at hand, content may be connected to personal knowledge, to schooling or technical knowledge, or to social or community knowledge. Any given language event is likely to encompass some combination of personal, academic, and social knowledge.

The *purpose* dimension addresses the question of why we use language. In other words, it considers the range of motives, reasons, and desired outcomes, or the ends to which we direct our literacy practices. We all use language for a variety of purposes, such as to learn, to express ideas, to convey information, to persuade others, to note things we observe, to savor aesthetic experience, or to engage with others socially. Again, any given literacy event may involve several of these different purposes.

The *development* dimension focuses on how learners develop competencies in the language arts. Students grow as language users by building a knowledge of content, a repertoire of strategies (such as predicting, synthesizing, reflecting, and identifying words and their meanings), and the ability to apply these flexibly as they engage in various types of literacy activities.

As students progress through their formal schooling, they grow in their ability to use language clearly, strategically, critically, and creatively. They discover the rich assortment of ways in which they can use language to pursue their own goals and purposes. They develop a knowledge of the conventions of language and the capacity to apply this knowledge. They learn to integrate their knowledge of text with their own experiences, enriching what they bring to each literacy event.

Because contextual variables influence all areas of learning, the graphic presents context encircling the other three dimensions of this model. Social and cultural contexts, in particular, shape linguistic patterns, meanings, and uses. The standards do not focus explicitly on context because, as we noted earlier, we leave the particulars of curricular definition in the hands of local educators—and that is one place where context comes into play. We wish to affirm the importance of authentic learning experiences involving a variety of contexts, however. As teachers, students, parents, and policymakers articulate curricula, instruction, and assessment processes, they should generate learning opportunities that respond to local needs and interests.

While each of these dimensions of the language learning model can be viewed independently, each also overlaps with the others. The intersections of the content, purpose, and development circles in the figure reflect the profound interrelation of *what, why,* and *how* in English language arts learning. Our standards concentrate primarily on the content dimension (as we will discuss in the following chapter), but the other dimensions are always present. To put it differently, within each standard, content issues—such as the appropriate range and depth of reading materials—are closely linked to purpose and developmental processes. In the remainder of this chapter, we consider each aspect of our perspective.

We believe that students will best develop their knowledge, skills, and competencies through meaningful experiences and instruction that recognize purpose, form, and content as inextricably interrelated.

CONTENT

Every text experience we have—every work we read, see, hear, or create—expands what we bring to future literacy experiences. Accordingly, the development of literacy and the attainment of the English language arts standards set forth in this document depend on experience with and systematic study of a wide array of texts, visual and spoken as well as written.

Although we do not believe it is productive to dictate a specific English language arts curriculum that should be enacted in every classroom or every school, it is important to define broadly the content that students need to know in order to become informed, confident, and competent users of language. That we discuss this knowledge base separately here does not mean that content and skills should be taught separately from one another. We believe, on the contrary, that students will best develop their knowledge, skills, and competencies through meaningful experiences and instruction that recognize purpose, form, and content as inextricably interrelated.

Standards for the English Language Arts

What are the essential elements of the knowledge base for the English language arts? All students need to know about and work with a broad range of texts, spoken and visual as well as written. They must develop a repertoire of processes or strategies for creating, interpreting, and analyzing texts. And they need to know about the underlying systems and structures of language. Let us examine each of these areas in turn.

A Broad Range of Texts

Language learning depends on the exploration and careful study of a wide array of texts. In particular, students need to read literature, including classic, contemporary, and popular narratives, poems, songs, and plays. Exploring literary worlds gives students a new perspective on their own experience and enables them to discover how literature can capture the richness and complexity of human life.

Broad reading also includes informational and academic texts, such as textbooks, lab manuals, papers, and reference materials; student-produced texts, including peer writing, journals, and student newspapers and literary magazines; technological resources, such as computer software, computer networks, databases, CD-ROMs, and laser disks; mass media and other visual texts, including films, selected television programs, magazines, and newspapers; socially significant oral and written texts, such as speeches, radio and television broadcasts, political documents, editorials, and advertisements; and everyday texts, such as letters, bulletin board notices, memos, and signs.

Although it is important to study some texts in detail, a primary goal should be for students to understand and enjoy texts and to explore diverse works independently. Students also need opportunities to compare the ways in which ideas and information are presented in different media—for example, the ways in which a narrative differs when read, heard, or viewed on film.

Additionally, students need to know about the literary traditions that contextualize literary texts and about properties of the genres they represent. They should realize, for example, that reading a literary text involves some different processes and different background knowledge than reading an informational text. Understanding the generic and formal constraints in informational texts (for example, the use of headings, graphic aids and other design elements, and the conventions of standard written English) is also an essential part of students' knowledge. Further, students need to develop some understanding of the underlying systems and structures of texts and of the visual and linguistic systems out of which texts are created.

Processes and Strategies

In addition to knowledge of texts and text features, students need to learn an array of processes and strategies for comprehending and producing texts. These include, for example, the use of background knowledge to construct meaning, effective strategies for fluently identifying words, study strategies to enhance learning and recall, and systematic processes for approaching writing. By *strategies,* we mean practiced but flexible ways of responding to recognizable contexts, situations, or demands. Because no one reading strategy, study technique, or writing process is best for all students, it is inappropriate to teach a single way of approaching all language tasks. However, we have the responsibility to use the best available research and knowledge based on careful observations to recommend those instructional processes and materials that promote the development of language arts capabilities.

These aspects of knowledge and understanding are, we believe, critical to the development of students' competencies in the English language arts. The following chapter discusses these various aspects of knowledge and experience in greater detail, within the context of defining the standards.

Systems and Structures of Language

Another critical part of students' English language arts education involves the study of the systems and structures of language and of language conventions, including grammar, punctuation, and spelling. In addition to gaining competency in these aspects of language use, students need to understand how language conventions vary from one context to another. In other words, they need to know how to apply their knowledge of the systems and structures of language depending on the nature of the task at hand. This requires experience in creating texts for a range of audiences and purposes. As students become experienced at composing different types of texts, they learn to adapt their language to different audiences and to other contextual variables.

PURPOSE

A strong grasp of content in the English language arts is vital, but knowledge alone is of little value if one has no need to, or cannot, apply it. The ability to use language for a variety of purposes is therefore another essential part of the learning experience. We believe that a central goal of English language arts education is to ensure that students are able to use language to address their own needs as well as the needs of their families, their communities, and the greater society. In particular, we recommend a focus in English language arts education on four purposes of language use: for obtaining and communicating information, for literary response and expression, for learning and reflection, and for problem solving and application.

For Obtaining and Communicating Information

Nonfiction, informational books, magazine articles, documentary films, encyclopedia entries on paper or CD-ROM, catalogs, interviews, recordings of news broadcasts, schedules, and instructions—we use all of these types of texts to get information about topics that interest us or to find out something we need to know. Similarly, we create many different kinds of texts to convey information to others, ranging from diagrams, verbal directions, and simple reports on observations of natural phenomena to laboratory reports and multimedia research projects. By learning to use many different media—traditional and nontraditional, print and nonprint—to collect and convey information, students become aware of the range of possibilities available to them for communicating with others. Building on the information-gathering and presentation skills that students use routinely in everyday life, teachers can strengthen students' ability to perform more complex and challenging tasks and to enhance their learning in other curriculum areas.

Children learn language and its uses simultaneously.
—Frank Smith

For Literary Response and Expression

Literary response and expression are aesthetic acts involving complex interactions of emotion and intellect. The acts of responding to, interpreting, and creating literary texts enable us to participate in other lives and worlds beyond our own and to reflect on who we are. In order to interpret and create, students need to understand what makes a text literary. We use the word *literary* broadly here, to mean the imaginative treatment of a subject using language and text structure that is inventive and often multilayered.

From this perspective, students' literary experiences should be extensive. Students should learn that virtually any type of text—essay, diary, or film, as well as sonnet, short story, or play—can contain powerful literary expression. Similarly, students need opportunities to compose many different types of texts that draw on their imaginations and involve the use of literary language. Such experiences enhance students' understanding and appreciation of the literary texts they read as part of their schoolwork and as their chosen leisure reading.

For Learning and Reflection

Language is a powerful instrument for learning and reflection, and students who are encouraged to use their literacy skills to pursue their own interests and questions are likely to discover this potential. From this perspective, language enables us to communicate not only with and for others, but also with and for ourselves.

Students need frequent opportunities to talk and write as learners and thinkers. Student journals and small-group discussions may be especially productive in this regard. By engaging in these types of activities, and by discussing their reflections with others, students develop a sense of their own resourcefulness and of the possibilities that language makes available to them, and are better able to set and work toward their own goals. Such activities also provide their teachers with valuable insights into their students' learning.

For Problem Solving and Application

Students use language every day to solve problems and grapple with issues that concern them. To respond to these situations and demands, students need to be able to use language to pose significant questions, to become informed, to obtain and communicate information, and to think critically and creatively. Purposeful language use demands all of these capacities.

Whether they are reading instructions in order to make a model airplane, applying conflict resolution strategies to negotiate the use of a toy, writing a letter to the police to report a stolen bicycle, or writing a new script for an online role-playing game, students routinely use language for problem solving in everyday life. The challenge facing teachers is to draw on students' real needs for language and to use these as a platform for motivating further learning and strengthening of their competencies.

DEVELOPMENT

The dimension of development—the question of how students should be able to use language—incorporates two distinct issues. The first concerns how students acquire knowledge and how they develop competencies with practice over time. This developmental dimension is emphasized in our discussion of "learning how to learn" (in Chapter 1), and is incorporated in many of the individual standards. The second issue focuses on performance and relates to the quality of students' performance over time. In particular it addresses the need for students to learn to use language clearly, strategically, critically, and creatively.

During their preschool years, young learners move toward literacy in a number of remarkable ways. Their language development starts at birth as they begin to hear language, process it, and construct meaning with it. Young children who see people around them engaging in literacy behaviors are curious; they see what language can do, and they want to participate in these forms of communication. As they listen to stories and nonfiction books that are read to them, young children begin to build appreciation for books as a source of enjoyment and learning, to discover different literary genres, and to develop their language abilities. Sharing books with children also instills in them a sense of story and a sensitivity to the writing styles found in expository texts. Through these experiences, children develop an understanding that spoken words are composed of a limited number of identifiable units or sounds (phonemic awareness), and that the letters of the alphabet represent sounds in speech (the alphabetic principle). In time, with this accumulation of literacy experiences and knowledge, young children begin to use reading and writing to express their ideas and needs.

As children move through the elementary and middle school grades, their reading and writing experiences expand their understanding of the importance of literacy in their lives. They often develop preferences for specific types of books and read deeply within those they most favor. Their writing experiences help them find their own voices and realize that writing gives them new communicative powers. Additionally, they develop a wide range of strategies to draw upon in their reading and writing activities.

Similarly, older readers, such as high school students reading sonnets for the first time or learning the technical language of subjects such as physics or calculus, continue to discover and learn to use new words and new forms of language through the practice of reading and writing. Thus, language learning is a dynamic and lifelong process through which individuals develop and fine-tune an expanding repertoire of capacities for communicating with others and with themselves.

How Students Acquire Knowledge and Develop Competency over Time

According to this integrative perspective of literacy development, all language learners—whether they are infants just beginning to speak, older children learning to read and write, or adults acquiring a second language or a new professional vocabulary—learn language by using it purposefully and negotiating with others. Language users "make" meaning, constantly revising their initial understandings of what they read, hear, view, and create in light of what they learn from subsequent reading, listening, viewing, and creating. In other words, the processes of language use are active, not passive. We learn language not simply for the sake of learning language; we learn it to make sense of the world around us and to communicate our understandings with others. In fact, as we discuss in the following section, language cannot be divorced from the social contexts in which it occurs.

This view of language development has clear and profound implications for teaching and learning. If we accept that language development occurs through purposeful use, then English language arts instruction must nurture this development by giving students the opportunity to engage in a wide array of experiences with language, and it must ensure that students perceive the value of these experiences.

Development also implies a progression in students' competency and sophistication. While this aspect of development clearly informs the perspective on learning presented here, it is important to contrast this integrative perspective with an incremental or grade-level view of student progress. While we present a number of dimensions along which students' development may be seen and evaluated, we do not attempt to specify levels of achievement corresponding to grade level or age. These criteria are best defined locally, in the contexts of specific schools and students' needs.

Furthermore, instructional approaches will not be the same for all students because their experiences with literacy before entering school will not have been the same. Children who have been read to frequently, for example, will have a rich understanding of some of the basics of print literacy, including the direction of the print, the fronts and backs of books, and, most fundamental, the awareness that the squiggles or marks on the page represent sounds, words, or concepts in the language they already know. Children with limited preschool exposure to reading may be less familiar with these concepts. Even so, they possess a large repertoire of

We learn language not simply for the sake of learning language; we learn it to make sense of the world around us and to communicate our understandings with others.

images and background knowledge that provides a base for learning, and through meaningful instruction and experience they will be able to build on their understandings. Their listening and speaking vocabularies will expand and form a stronger foundation for reading and writing. They will begin to examine books more carefully and build an appreciation for reading for enjoyment and information. They will see drawing and writing as ways of communicating through marks made on paper and begin to attend to the forms of letters and to sounds; with support and instruction, they will come to understand the alphabetic principle—that written letters can be used to represent sounds.

The first step in literacy education, then, is not to assume, as has been done too frequently in the past, either that all students bring a common core of literacy knowledge to school, or that those who do not bring what is customarily expected are deficient. Rather, the first step is to respect each student's home language, prior knowledge, and cultural experience, and to determine what he or she already knows and can do upon entering school. Teachers must then provide appropriate and rich instructional support on that basis.

How Students Should Be Able to Use Language

A second issue connected to development is more directly related to performance. This issue has to do with how students should be able to use language. Several criteria for this are discussed below.

Clearly

Students need to be able to use language clearly and fluently—with precision and accuracy. Audience and purpose are important considerations in deciding the form that communication needs to take. For example, clarity can be achieved in face-to-face conversation with family members through unelaborated language, while class discussions or conversations with public audiences may call for more complete elaboration.

In interpreting texts, students need to be able to use various types of cues to derive a clear understanding of the range of possible meanings. Students should learn to respect the integrity of a text, and to generate hypotheses and inferences drawn from it. And in composing texts and visual representations, students should be able to define audience, purpose, and context; then, drawing on their knowledge of the systems and structures of language, they should be able to organize and express their ideas clearly and precisely.

Strategically

Students need to be able to use a wide range of strategies (including predicting, hypothesizing, estimating, drafting, synthesizing, and identifying words and their meanings) to interpret and create various types of texts. This entails sensitivity to the purpose, nature, and audience of a text, and an ability to use this awareness to adapt language accordingly. Such flexibility is vital, for assembling a collection of strategies is of little use without a knowledge of how and when to apply them.

When a student reaches an impasse and finds that his or her current strategies are not working, the teacher has an opportunity to help that student learn new ones. At such times, motivation to discover alternative approaches is usually very high. By giving learners a wide range of language experiences, particularly experiences that are interesting and challenging to them, teachers are most likely to help students see the value of having an array of strategies and the ability to use them flexibly in various language activities.

Critically

Critical language users question and comment on what they read, hear, and view. Students' critical skills are nurtured in classrooms where questioning, brainstorming, hypothesizing, reflecting, and imaging are encouraged and rewarded. Students develop the ability to pose questions as they read, listen, and view: What inferences can I draw from this text? What perspective does this text ask me to assume? What viewpoint is presented in this text? What does this text omit or distort? How is my own response related to what is presented by the text?

Critical language users bring original ways of thinking and novel interpretations to texts. While critical thinking is often concerned with making distinctions and marking differences, effective critical thinkers also draw connections among texts, their own responses to them, various bodies of knowledge, and their own experiences. Development of critical language skills enables students to provide informed opinions about texts they encounter, and to support their interpretations with multiple forms of evidence.

Students' critical skills are nurtured in classrooms where questioning, brainstorming, hypothesizing, reflecting, and imaging are encouraged and rewarded.

Creatively

Students use language creatively when they are encouraged to stretch or reimagine received forms and vocabularies, or to invent new ones, to embody their own ideas. In composing their texts, creative language users pursue imaginative risks, departing from established conventions and well-worn formulations. Like critical thinkers, creative language users draw on their experiences, personal observations, strategies, and prior knowledge as they explore the boundaries of texts and forms. They move beyond surface meanings and appreciate the complexities and nuances of language.

CONTEXT

Regardless of whether we are reading or writing, speaking or listening, viewing or visually representing, a context always surrounds any activity. If we are composing a letter, for example, we consider our audience. To whom are we writing, and how does this influence the ideas and language we choose? Other contextual variables are at play, too, including our level of motivation and

interest. If we are listening to a presentation, contextual variables include our perceptions of the speaker and our prior knowledge about what is being communicated.

Perhaps one of the most influential aspects of context is the social dimension. Many illustrations of reading and writing show one person alone, looking intently downward at a text or a paper, deeply immersed in thought. But we are coming to realize how fundamentally social the process of becoming literate is. Saying that language development is social does not mean that the process has no private dimensions. Indeed, all of us draw on our own sets of experiences and strategies as we use language to construct meanings from what we read, write, hear, say, observe, and represent. These specific meanings are individual and personal. Yet the range of possible meanings that we can discover and know is, to a great extent, socially determined. What we can know is much influenced by what those in our language community know and by our shared experiences and shared texts.

Perhaps the most obvious way in which language is social is that it almost always relates to others, either directly or indirectly: we speak to others, listen to others, write to others, read what others have written, make visual representations for others, and interpret their visual representations. Doing so also helps us clarify our ideas for ourselves, but what nourishes language growth is participation in language communities. As we grow and move in ever-broadening social situations, we become participants in an increasing number of language groups that necessarily influence the ways in which we speak, write, and represent.

Language development is also social in that we use a system of shared conventions to communicate with one another and to create new language. We interact using the conventions accepted in the different language communities in which we operate, and these shared conventions make communication possible within and among these different groups. At the same time, these conventions are always changing, as new metaphors and terms are invented to reflect new ideas and experiences.

We know, of course, that our students come from many different language communities. This is especially evident in classrooms where students speak a range of languages as well as different varieties of the language we call English. Recent research on actual language use shows, moreover, that no single "standard" of English exists around the world, or even within a single country. All of us who speak English speak different varieties of English depending on whom we are communicating with, the circumstances involved, the purpose of the exchange, and other factors. Indeed,

Standards for the English Language Arts

creative and communicative powers are enhanced when students develop and maintain multiple language competencies.

Nonetheless, some varieties of English are more useful than others for higher education, for employment, and for participation in what the Conference on College Composition and Communication (1993) in a language policy statement calls "the language of wider communication." Therefore, although we respect the diversity in spoken and written English, we believe that all students should learn this language of wider communication.

■   ■   ■

In summary, the perspective informing the English language arts standards places the learner at the center. The content dimension of the graphic presented in Figure 1 addresses what students should know and be able to do with respect to the English language arts. The purpose dimension addresses the question of why we use language, and the development dimension focuses on how learners develop competencies in the language arts. Because context influences all areas of learning, this dimension encircles all three of the preceding areas.

Although it is illuminating to focus on these dimensions of language learning separately, it is important to emphasize the complex interactions that exist among them. Each dimension of language learning overlaps with the others, as the graphic illustrates. As noted earlier in this chapter, the English language arts standards focus primarily on the content dimension, defining what we expect students to know and be able to do with respect to language. Invariably in any language event, however, purpose, development, and context are also intertwined.

As we see in the following chapter, this perspective on language learning can be used to discuss overarching concerns and themes in the set of standards as a whole. Further, it provides a way to examine each particular standard in detail, through the lenses of content, purpose, and development.

REFERENCE

Conference on College Composition and Communication. (1993). *The National Language Policy.* [Brochure]. Urbana, IL: NCTE.

CHAPTER 3 THE ENGLISH LANGUAGE ARTS STANDARDS

The standards presented in this chapter define what we believe students should know and be able to do in the English language arts. As the preceding chapters have made clear, we believe that these standards should articulate a consensus growing out of actual classroom practices, and not be a prescriptive framework. If the standards work, then teachers will recognize their students, themselves, their goals, and their daily endeavors in this document; so, too, will they be inspired, motivated, and provoked to reevaluate some of what they do in class. By engaging with these standards, teachers will, we hope, also think and talk energetically about the assumptions that underlie their own classroom practices and those of their colleagues.

The standards reflect some of the best ideas already at work in English language arts education around the country. Because language and the language arts continue to evolve and grow, our standards must remain provisional enough to leave room for future developments in the field. And it is important to reemphasize that these standards are meant to be suggestive, not exhaustive. Ideally, teachers, parents, administrators, and students will use them as starting points for an ongoing discussion about classroom activities and curricula.

The primary focus of the standards is on the content of English language arts learning. As we noted in the preceding chapter, content cannot be separated from the purpose, development, and context of language learning. As educators translate these standards into practice, they must consider the unique range of purposes, developmental processes, and contexts that exists in their communities.

The twelve content standards for the English language arts follow. Let us reflect briefly on the group as a whole before moving into more specific elaborations of each in turn.

The act of setting out a list like this one implies that knowledge and understanding can be sliced into tidy and distinct categories, but obviously literacy learning (like any other area of human learning) is far more complicated than that. We acknowledge the complex relationships that exist among the standards. Further, we do not mean to imply that the standards can or should be translated into isolated components of instruction. On the contrary: virtually any instructional activity is likely to address multiple standards simultaneously. Nor is the order of arrangement and numbering of

IRA/NCTE
STANDARDS FOR THE ENGLISH LANGUAGE ARTS

The vision guiding these standards is that all students must have the opportunities and resources to develop the language skills they need to pursue life's goals and to participate fully as informed, productive members of society. These standards assume that literacy growth begins before children enter school as they experience and experiment with literacy activities—reading and writing, and associating spoken words with their graphic representations. Recognizing this fact, these standards encourage the development of curriculum and instruction that make productive use of the emerging literacy abilities that children bring to school. Furthermore, the standards provide ample room for the innovation and creativity essential to teaching and learning. They are not prescriptions for particular curriculum or instruction.

Although we present these standards as a list, we want to emphasize that they are not distinct and separable; they are, in fact, interrelated and should be considered as a whole.

1. Students read a wide range of print and nonprint texts to build an understanding of texts, of themselves, and of the cultures of the United States and the world; to acquire new information; to respond to the needs and demands of society and the workplace; and for personal fulfillment. Among these texts are fiction and nonfiction, classic and contemporary works.

2. Students read a wide range of literature from many periods in many genres to build an understanding of the many dimensions (e.g., philosophical, ethical, aesthetic) of human experience.

3. Students apply a wide range of strategies to comprehend, interpret, evaluate, and appreciate texts. They draw on their prior experience, their interactions with other readers and writers, their knowledge of word meaning and of other texts, their word identification strategies, and their understanding of textual features (e.g., sound-letter correspondence, sentence structure, context, graphics).

4. Students adjust their use of spoken, written, and visual language (e.g., conventions, style, vocabulary) to communicate effectively with a variety of audiences and for different purposes.

5. Students employ a wide range of strategies as they write and use different writing process elements appropriately to communicate with different audiences for a variety of purposes.

6. Students apply knowledge of language structure, language conventions (e.g., spelling and punctuation), media techniques, figurative language, and genre to create, critique, and discuss print and nonprint texts.

7. Students conduct research on issues and interests by generating ideas and questions, and by posing problems. They gather, evaluate, and synthesize data from a variety of sources (e.g., print and nonprint texts, artifacts, people) to communicate their discoveries in ways that suit their purpose and audience.

8. Students use a variety of technological and informational resources (e.g., libraries, databases, computer networks, video) to gather and synthesize information and to create and communicate knowledge.

9. Students develop an understanding of and respect for diversity in language use, patterns, and dialects across cultures, ethnic groups, geographic regions, and social roles.

10. Students whose first language is not English make use of their first language to develop competency in the English language arts and to develop understanding of content across the curriculum.

11. Students participate as knowledgeable, reflective, creative, and critical members of a variety of literacy communities.

12. Students use spoken, written, and visual language to accomplish their own purposes (e.g., for learning, enjoyment, persuasion, and the exchange of information).

the standards meant to suggest any progression or hierarchy. Numbering them simply makes it easier to refer to them concisely in discussion.

Readers will recognize that these standards can be grouped into clusters. Standards 1 and 2, for example, discuss the range of materials that students should read and their purposes for reading; the former emphasizes breadth and diversity of texts, while the latter concentrates on literary works. Like Standards 1 and 2, Standard 3 also concerns reading, but it addresses reading strategies or processes rather than texts. This third standard also relates to Standard 4; both emphasize the importance of students' knowledge of language use, variation, and conventions.

Standards 5 and 6 work together to move from reading and comprehending to creating texts. Both discuss the types of knowledge that students need in order to use language effectively as writers, speakers, or visual representers. Both of these standards also emphasize the connections between reading and writing and the importance of gaining a working knowledge of language structure and conventions. The next pair of standards, 7 and 8, concern research and inquiry. Standard 7 stresses student approaches to inquiry, while Standard 8 concentrates on the use of research materials, with particular attention to new, technologically driven modes of research and data synthesis.

The evolving needs of America's students—whose growing ethnic and linguistic diversity is changing the social makeup of contemporary classrooms—are taken up in Standards 9 and 10. Taken together, these standards suggest that a multicultural language arts curriculum is both useful and necessary today, offering students the language resources they will need to participate in the nation and world of tomorrow.

The last two standards build on the vital recognition that literacy has both social and personal significance for language users. Standard 11 stresses the use of collaborative learning as a way for students to use the language arts to find and develop a sense of community. In Standard 12, students, motivated by their own goals, learn that the language arts can help them discover a sense of their individuality as well.

Readers will find other ways of linking these standards: the issue of new technology, for example, addressed explicitly in Standard 8, on research materials, is also a central theme in the discussion of literacy communities in number 11. Student-directed learning, a theme throughout many of the standards, explicitly links numbers 7, 10, and 11. The structures and conventions of language, a central topic in all of the language arts, form a key focus in Standards 3, 4, 6, and 9.

We encourage readers to reflect upon other ways in which these standards are connected, and to think through the elaborations of the individual standards using the lens provided by the graphic discussed in Chapter 2. That perspective may be used to explore the interplay of content, purpose, development, and context within each of the standards, and it serves to remind us of the central importance of the individual learner in all of them. Much as the dimension of context encircles our language learning model, so we hope teachers and other readers of these standards will draw on their own knowledge and experience, and the salient needs in their own educational communities, to enrich and expand the brief elaborations offered below.

Reading is a wonderfully rich and complex human activity. It provokes reflection, introspection, and imaginative thinking and allows us to create and explore new ideas.

Standards for the English Language Arts

THE STANDARDS
IN DETAIL

1 *Students read a wide range of print and nonprint texts to build an understanding of texts, of themselves, and of the cultures of the United States and the world; to acquire new information; to respond to the needs and demands of society and the workplace; and for personal fulfillment. Among these texts are fiction and nonfiction, classic and contemporary works.*

Reading is a wonderfully rich and complex human activity. It provokes reflection, introspection, and imaginative thinking and allows us to create and explore new ideas. It introduces us to different representations of the world. It fills our needs for information and communication and enables us to learn about different subjects, perform various tasks, participate in the workplace, and understand and evaluate our place in the world. It also gives us the intrinsic pleasure of linguistic and imaginative activity.

Even before they enter school, children can learn to enjoy books and other print material. Listening to storybooks instills a sense of story and familiarizes children with different literary genres. In school, as they read, respond to, and study a variety of texts, students become deeply engaged with language and construct rich, personal meanings from what they read. Knowledge of and about different types of texts gives students an orientation, a set of expectations, that they can bring to each new text they encounter. For example, some students just entering school, especially those who have not been read to regularly, learn to use and understand new ways for talking about stories they hear and stories they themselves read and write. They must think about "what happens next" and "how characters feel" and "why an author makes choices." In a similar fashion, older students may learn to expect that an experimental film may deliver a nonlinear plot; that greater suspension of disbelief is required in listening to classmates tell fantasy stories than in hearing them describe a family holiday; that some short stories begin with flashbacks; and that political speeches require watchfulness for one-sided arguments.

Through discussion of what they read and through their own extensive reading, students also learn that any given text can be understood in a variety of ways, depending on the context. African folk narratives or Greek myths, for instance, can be read as delightful, entertaining stories, as representations of mythic archetypes, or as cultural, religious, or philosophical histories of particular regions or people. Reading activities often invite several types of understanding simultaneously. Equally important, readers often read for several purposes—some internal, such as personal growth, and some external, such as finding out new information and ideas.

Because there are many kinds of reading and many purposes for reading, students need to read for a range of purposes and within a variety of contexts in order to become proficient and knowledgeable readers. They need opportunities to explore and study many different kinds of printed texts, including contemporary and traditional novels, newspaper and magazine articles, poems, nonfiction works on a range of subjects, historical documents from family and community sources, reference materials, children's and young adult books and magazines, popular journals, biographies, autobiographies, journals, and letters. Students should also read work by other students: writers and readers build self-confidence and respect for one another by reading and studying their peers' work.

Nonprint texts are also an essential part of students' reading experience. Students need to make effective use of a range of spoken texts, both formal and informal, ranging from speeches and plays to word games and playful talk. Opportunities to study and create visual texts—including narrative and documentary films, television, advertisements, maps, illustrations, multimedia/CD resources, and other graphic displays—are also crucial. Graphic and visual messages influence contemporary society powerfully, and students need to learn how the elements of visual language communicate ideas and shape thought and action.

What criteria should be used to select particular works for classroom study? In choosing texts, teachers and students should consider relevance to students' interests and other readings; relevance for students' roles in society and the workplace; literary quality; and balance and variety in form, style, and content. Complexity is another important criterion. Students benefit from reading texts that challenge and provoke them; they also benefit from simpler texts that promote fluency. Opportunities to read books for pleasure are also vital. While some of these texts will be suggested or assigned by teachers, students also need to choose texts for themselves so that they develop a sense of themselves as independent readers. As they discuss their reading selections with their teachers and peers, students gain insight into their reading preferences and learn to evaluate the importance of different kinds of texts.

The works that students read should also reflect the diversity of the United States' population in terms of gender, age, social class, religion, and ethnicity. Students' understanding of our society and its history—and their ability to recognize and appreciate difference and diversity—are expanded when they read primary texts from across a wide demographic spectrum.

It is not enough to read a variety of works, however; students also need to discover the connections among them. Teachers can help students to discover these textual relationships by assembling clusters of readings that focus on a single theme or event but that cut across boundaries of geography, community, and genre. In one New Hampshire middle school, for example, students engaged in an interdisciplinary learning project centered on Katherine Paterson's *Lyddie*, a historical novel about young girls working in nineteenth-century New England textile mills. Supplementary texts included women's letters from the period, historical writing on the economics of millwork, and Dr. Seuss's *The Lorax*. Similarly, students in an Iowa high school read Twain's *Adventures of Huckleberry Finn* and explored connections to other novels of the period, to the political issues of the time, and to the geography of the Mississippi River itself. Such learning experiences allow students to form a colorful portrait of their region and to value reading as a source of important information and new insights.

Wallace Stegner observed that there are only two disciplines whose subject matter must be accumulative: history and literature. . . . The farther time extends, the more literary works . . . that are published, the more difficult it becomes to agree on a literary core for the curriculum. . . . If agreement is to come on what should be taught to whom and to what ends, that agreement must take place at local rather than state or national levels, for only at that level can teachers take into full account the problems, interests, and abilities of the students they daily face.

—Ed Farrell,
Journal of Teaching Writing

Standards for the English Language Arts

Through experience with texts, students deepen their knowledge not only of themselves but also of the world. Self-discovery and cultural awareness are intertwined. Extensive and varied reading provides a lens through which to view and critique American and world history and contemporary social life. Thus, as students read widely, and as they discuss and reflect on what they read, they develop an understanding of themselves both as individuals and as parts of a larger social whole. Their literacy skills and their social knowledge grow together.

2 *Students read a wide range of literature from many periods in many genres to build an understanding of the many dimensions (e.g., philosophical, ethical, aesthetic) of human experience.*

The texts that we call "literary" have a special function in our culture and in student learning. Literary works are valuable not just as informative or communicative vehicles, but as artistic creations and representations of human culture at particular times and in particular places. They are a living archive of a history of philosophical, ethical, and aesthetic thought. As students learn to read and respond to literary texts, they discover the special features of these texts, and they develop the special skills and vocabulary needed to experience and appreciate literature fully, in all its various forms. They learn, for example, that literary language is rich with metaphor, imagery, rhyme, and other figures and devices.

Accordingly, students need to read and study literary texts in a variety of genres, including poetry, short stories, novels, plays, essays, biographies, and autobiographies. Narrative in its many forms can be introduced early, through picture books, puppet shows, role-playing, and story time. There is strong evidence that when young children hear repeated readings of favorite books, their responses to all books become more complex. Young students can learn about drama, too, through live action, dialogue games, and visual media. Poetry and rhyme help young readers connect sounds to words and help them enjoy the 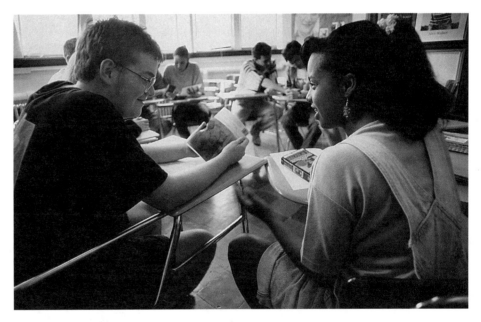 musical, rhythmic qualities of language. As students grow in literary experience, they discover the qualities of various genres—for example, how poems share certain uses of language and sound, how novels develop characters and plot, and how plays establish and resolve dramatic tension.

Students who read literature learn that literary texts are often relevant to their own lives. Their exploration of literary worlds also offers perspectives which may contrast and conflict with their own experiences and invite them to reflect critically on alternative ways of knowing and being.

A literary education consists of classic literary texts like Shakespeare's *Romeo and Juliet,* Hinton's *The Outsiders,* Hurston's *Their Eyes Were Watching God,* Brown's *Goodnight Moon,* or White's *Charlotte's Web,* as well as more recent works like Paterson's *The Great Gilly Hopkins,* Cormier's *I Am the Cheese,* Mochizuki's *Baseball Saved Us,* or Greenfield's *Grandmama's Joy.* Both classic and contemporary works are essential to a literary education.

Students' experiences of literary texts are made richer when they are familiar with the specialized terms and concepts of literary analysis. Each literary genre has its own formal qualities, and students benefit from studying these conventions. Young children who have been read to extensively reflect their understanding of literary conventions in two ways. First, when they "read" or retell a story, their language may take on a distinctly literary style, indicating that they understand the difference between conversation and "book talk." Second, beginning writers often use conventions such as "once upon a time" or "the end" to mark their early compositions as stories, rather than as letters or informational pieces. Similarly, focusing on the structure of the sonnet and haiku in the context of reading a variety of different poems allows more experienced readers to discover connections between theme and form. By studying various text genres in detail—for example, science fiction—students learn to recognize their unique features and to see connections across texts within a given genre. These studies enable students to learn how literary works are constructed, how they share certain artistic forms, and what makes each a distinct work.

Many literary texts—not just fiction, but also essays, other prose works, plays, and poems—give students opportunities to engage in ethical and philosophical reflection on the values and beliefs of their own cultures, of other cultures, and of other times and places. They show how individuals discover the significance of inner experience, social life, and history as they find their place in the world. In many of our most important literary works, authors depict moral conflicts as characters struggle to know themselves, to make decisions, and to act within a larger society. Students who explore the moral and ethical dimensions of literature see that reading can deepen their understanding of the complexities of human life, often affirming their own experiences or casting them in a new light. Literacy thus can become not just a means to an end, but an exploration in which students' own worlds and experiences open themselves to those of many others.

Because literary texts enable students to envision and explore worlds (both actual and imagined) from perspectives other than their own, they help students to imagine and challenge different worlds. Students who have learned, through literary texts, to view their own lives and the world around them in new and different ways are more apt to consider alternatives rather than simply accepting things as they are. Literature thus plays a vital role in the development of critical thinking. Through literary reading, students learn to think about and to question their own perspectives; they learn to assume different, critical stances toward events, circumstances, and issues. Readers of literature come to recognize and evaluate human experiences as well as the literature in which those experiences are represented.

Many literary texts give students opportunities to engage in ethical and philosophical reflection on the values and beliefs of their own cultures, of other cultures, and of other times and places.

Standards for the English Language Arts

3 *Students apply a wide range of strategies to comprehend, interpret, evaluate, and appreciate texts. They draw on their prior experience, their interactions with other readers and writers, their knowledge of word meaning and of other texts, their word identification strategies, and their understanding of textual features (e.g., sound-letter correspondence, sentence structure, context, graphics).*

Before even beginning the first sentence of a text, knowledgeable readers know how to approach and frame a reading experience with a sense of purpose, need, and direction. Becoming a knowledgeable reader, however, takes time and many experiences with different kinds of texts. Young learners soon recognize that they must orchestrate several different kinds of information in text. Drawing upon their sense of phonological awareness (their conscious awareness that spoken words can be broken into separate sounds and/or sound units), their knowledge of word meanings and language structure, and their knowledge of the world, they develop strategies for making meaning from many experiences with a variety of texts.

Students become knowledgeable readers by reading and studying a broad range of texts from which they learn to generalize the demands different genres place upon them as readers. As students learn to form expectations about a text, they become better able to decide which strategies they should use to comprehend, interpret, and evaluate what they are reading. Expectations may also enhance students' appreciation of texts and their personal responses to them.

Proficient readers also know how purpose affects their approach to a reading event. They know, for example, that studying the history of a region would involve a certain kind of reading if one were planning a vacation there, and quite another if one were writing a research report on the region's agriculture.

Effective readers also draw on their previous reading experiences as they delve into new works. For example, there are many mystery stories written for elementary school students. As young learners read these stories, they come to recognize the conventions of constructing mysteries, that is, how authors introduce clues and typically advance their plots. As they read more mysteries, younger readers begin to anticipate these conventions and use them to guide both their comprehension of the stories and their attempts to solve the mysteries. Later, they may use the same strategies with more complex and sophisticated examples of the genre. This understanding of the conventions of a specific genre is also useful in viewing mysteries on television or in the movies.

Although students come to recognize many of these expectations and strategies as they read and discuss related groups of texts, teacher explanation and modeling of reading strategies and independent conscious study also contribute to students' proficiency. Students need encouragement to think and talk about how they are creating meaning as they read and to pay close attention to the strategies they are using to do so. Reading is an active, recursive process in which readers make predictions based on linguistic and contextual cues (including the reader's knowledge of the world) and reevaluate those predictions in light of other cues. Students should

Based on what we now know, it is incorrect to suppose that there is a simple or single step, which, if taken correctly, will immediately allow a child to read. Becoming a skilled reader is a journey that involves many steps.

—*Becoming a Nation of Readers: The Report of the Commission on Reading* explore this meaning-making process explicitly, talking about how they move from predicting to confirming (or revising) their predictions, and back again. Thoughtful attention to their own cognitive processes will be rewarded with more complete and meaningful reading experiences and with an explicit sense of how to manage their own thinking.

In one Chicago kindergarten class, an opportunity to learn about reading and writing strategies emerged when a student brought a caterpillar to school. It had begun to form a chrysalis, and this inspired much conversation, wonder, and questioning among the students. A sign-in sheet and journal notebook were placed beside the caterpillar, in which students recorded their names (in whatever way they knew how) and drew or wrote their observations and questions. Students read and discussed what was real and what was fantasy in Eric Carle's *The Very Hungry Caterpillar* as a group. The teacher also provided a supply of related books, many with detailed pictures and charts about caterpillars, butterflies, and insects in general. These were displayed in the science corner for students' independent browsing. During this quiet reading time, the teacher listened to and monitored students' reading strategies, encouraging them to reflect on and learn from their miscues.

Using chart paper hung on the wall near the caterpillar, the teacher recorded students' responses to the Carle book, their observations of the caterpillar's metamorphosis, their conjectures about what would happen to the chrysalis, and their understandings and questions about butterflies. As the teacher listened to the students' comments, she often stopped to point out an interesting idea or word or to elicit learners' suggestions about how to spell a word or punctuate a sentence. On subsequent days, she and the students reviewed the charts both independently and together, much as they would enjoy a published "big book" displayed in their classroom. These sessions provided opportunities that were useful and relevant to students' level of emergent literacy.

Flexibility in applying different reading strategies is of the greatest importance: students need to know how to vary their approaches according to the nature of the text, the purpose of the reading, and their own knowledge and experience. If they are reading a text that uses familiar language, is in a familiar genre, or deals with a familiar topic, readers may proceed smoothly, rarely needing to stop to figure out a word or to question the use of certain rhetorical devices. On the other hand, if they are reading something that is especially challenging or foreign to them, they may need to pause frequently to search for graphic, phonological, syntactic, and semantic clues that will help them make sense of the text. Through practice and experience, students can learn to adapt or change the tactics they are using if they sense that things are not going well or if they move from one genre or context to another.

Further, students need to learn a variety of strategies for comprehending, interpreting, and analyzing spoken and visual language. If they are having a conversation with someone whose language patterns are very different from theirs, they may need to use a range of strategies (such as questioning, summarizing, and restating) to resolve ambiguities that arise. And if they are viewing a television program, they may ask themselves

Standards for the English Language Arts

about the purpose of the program—is it to communicate information, to entertain, or to persuade the audience to accept a certain point of view? Learning to be attentive to these different contexts enables students to move from basic comprehension to more sophisticated responses to what they are reading.

One of the most important functions of English language arts education is to help students learn to interpret texts—that is, to reflect on textual meaning from their own perspectives—and to evaluate texts—that is, to use critical thinking to identify particular text elements, such as logic, emotional appeal, and purpose. As students interpret and evaluate texts, they explore their own feelings, values, and responses to the ideas presented. Thus, they make their own responses to texts an integral part of their reading experience.

4 *Students adjust their use of spoken, written, and visual language (e.g., conventions, style, vocabulary) to communicate effectively with a variety of audiences and for different purposes.*

Throughout their lives, students will write and speak in widely differing social arenas: as informed citizens, as employees and co-workers, as neighbors. They will also use language as members of a family, for personal affirmation and reflection, and for cultural enrichment. In each instance, they will draw on their knowledge of language conventions as they adjust their speech and writing to respond to the needs of specific audiences, purposes, and situations. Therefore, students need to study how language conventions vary from one context to another. They need to make use of a range of language conventions as they create texts for different audiences and purposes.

Children's early writing plays an important part in their growth in language arts. Movement through phases of writing development—from scribbling to temporary spellings to conventional spellings—offers learners a variety of opportunities to make sense of how print communicates its message to a variety of audiences, for a variety of purposes. These initial efforts are unconventional by adult standards but they are important for the following reasons: They provide parents and teachers insights into how individual children construct meaning about why people write and about the process of writing. They also provide a valuable foundation for literacy growth. Through their drawing and scribbling, young learners convey their understanding that marks on paper communicate ideas and information. They begin to reflect their recognition of print as a means of communication—an important preliminary to the many ways they will use writing.

As they compose different types of works, students call on their knowledge of texts and text features. Again, audience is an especially important consideration. Writing in a diary, drafting an e-mail message to a grandparent, and requesting information from the chamber of commerce, for example, all involve different audiences and therefore different writing voices. Similarly, the informal, often fragmentary talk used among close friends gathered on the playground to discuss a basketball game is different from the more fully developed talk used with a teacher when discussing a piece of writing. While it may be perfectly appropriate to use personal language in a diary entry, doing so in an editorial for a school newspaper is likely to undermine readers' confidence in the author. Even handwriting can reflect a consideration of audience: scribbles may work when writing personal notes; however, directions to others on how to get to an unknown destination will most likely require clear and complete writing.

Individuals who are competent at communicating with others are sensitive to the needs of different audiences and to the ways in which the purpose of a communication shapes the kinds of ideas and information they choose and the way in which they present them. Depending on whether they are explaining something, arguing, persuading, or telling a story, good communicators have learned how to vary their organizational strategies. They adapt the level of detail they provide and the language they use according to the context of the communication. Students recognize, for example, that visual diagrams can help clarify difficult concepts, that a timeline may illustrate historical relationships, or that a colorful illustration may make a story more vivid for other readers. Through practice in making subtle (or not-so-subtle) strategic changes in style to fit different circumstances and audiences, students increase the likelihood that the texts they create will be understood and interpreted as they would like them to be.

Audience awareness is well illustrated in an elementary–high school collaboration in one Illinois school district. During a visit to an elementary school, students in one teacher's eleventh- and twelfth-grade classes interviewed third-grade students, asking about their hobbies, pets, favorite books, and other interests. The senior high students then composed original stories tailored for their elementary counterparts, getting responses at the drafting stage to assure that the stories were both lively and appropriate for their audience. Through this collaboration, both groups of students gained experience in communicating with a different audience and in exploring relationships between spoken and written texts.

To ensure that they can communicate effectively with a wide range of audiences, all students need to learn what we refer to as "the language of wider communication"—the forms of our language that are most commonly recognized as standard English. This does not imply that other varieties of English are somehow incorrect or invalid; rather, it means that all students need to have standard English in their repertoire of language forms, and to know when they should use it. When students engage in discussions of when and where this language of wider communication can and should be used, they further their knowledge of audience, purpose, and context, and in so doing discover something of the social significance of different language practices.

The social nature of language and communication is central to Standard 4. When students explore the connections between voice and audience, purpose and form, they become more versatile and confident in the choices they make as language users. Students who have experience communicating with a range of different audiences, moreover, are able to find a voice and style that are uniquely their own. As students adapt and modify their language to suit different purposes, they discover certain recurring phrases, devices, or images—the imprints of a personal style of communication.

If writing is thinking and discovery and selection and order and meaning, it is also awe and reverence and mystery and magic.
—Toni Morrison,
"The Site of Memory"

5   *Students employ a wide range of strategies as they write and use different writing process elements appropriately to communicate with different audiences for a variety of purposes.*

Just as students need an array of strategies for comprehending, interpreting, evaluating, and appreciating the texts written by others, so too do they need to apply an array of strategies as they write. Reading and writing are intertwined. Emergent writing efforts focus young learners' attention on details of text and reinforce beginning concepts about how print is produced. For example, these efforts strengthen learners' phonological awareness as they attempt to spell words they do not yet know but wish to write, thereby reinforcing understandings about letter-sound associations necessary for beginning reading. Other characteristics of good readers are also demonstrated by good writers: a sense of purpose, an ability to frame expectations of a task by drawing on prior writing experience, a knowledge of various approaches and how to apply them, the capacity to reflect on the writing process as it unfolds, and a willingness to change approaches in response to audience needs.

In order to attain these skills, students need frequent opportunities to write about different topics and for different audiences and purposes. Their own experiences, enriched by their readings and discussions with others in and out of school, are important resources for writing. For example, some highly rewarding writing was exchanged between high school students in Oklahoma City and Los Angeles when teachers in two schools set up e-mail communication between their classes. The Oklahoma students were able to formulate and express their emotional responses to the bombing in their city, and the Los Angeles students vividly described their experiences during the earthquake there. Not only was a sense of empathy generated between the classes, but the students also saw how writing could help them work through difficult and tangled emotions, and they practiced using written language to capture and repre-sent experience and memories for readers at a distance. Out of a desire to help each other understand and cope with traumatic experience, these students gained firsthand knowledge about the power of writing to connect people and to connect events in different parts of the world.

Students need guidance and practice to develop their skills in academic writing, whether they are responding to literary works or writing for other school subjects. They need to understand the varying demands of different kinds of writing tasks and to recognize how to adapt tone, style, and content for the particular task at hand. As with other aspects of learning, students' ability to create text—whether expressive or academic, formal or informal—is best developed through engagement in meaningful reading and writing activities. Students who write in the context of meaningful goals are more likely to work carefully to shape and revise what they compose. Teachers can create a sense of the purposefulness of writing by helping students to consider the needs of their audiences as they compose, edit, and revise.

As writers hear how different readers interpret and evaluate their work, they learn how to use constructive criticism to revise or recast their writing. This process helps students to internalize a sense of what their readers need and expect. It also extends the body of knowledge that they bring to future writing tasks, giving them greater confidence and versatility as writers.

In recent years many students have benefited from what is known as a "process approach" to writing instruction, which focuses on different activities typically involved in effective writing, such as planning, drafting, revising, editing, and publishing for real audiences. Unfortunately, this approach is sometimes translated into a highly structured sequence of activities, regardless of the task at hand. While it is certainly crucial for students to understand the repertoire of techniques involved in the writing process, it is equally important to teach them flexibility so that they know when to proceed step by step and when to adopt alternative strategies.

In reality, the writing process is recursive, not linear. Writers focus on many aspects of a task at once, some general and some particular: what ideas to incorporate, how to organize them, which words to choose, how to arrange them, where to insert commas. Writers move fluidly from whole to part and back again, shaping and defining their overall purpose as they develop specific examples and refine passages. They are problem-solvers, deciding as they go along how to tackle the many different challenges that arise.

To become confident and effective writers, then, students need to learn how to use various elements of writing flexibly and adaptively, shaping their approaches according to the purposes and audiences they have in mind. They need to be encouraged to try different approaches and to reconsider what they have written. In short, there is no such thing as one correct way of approaching writing. Effective student writers follow different strategies for different tasks, and they discover with each new task what works best.

6 *Students apply knowledge of language structure, language conventions (e.g., spelling and punctuation), media techniques, figurative language, and genre to create, critique, and discuss print and nonprint texts.*

To ensure that the texts they create are well received and understood by those who will be reading, viewing, or listening to them, students need a working knowledge of the systems and structures of language as well as familiarity with accepted language conventions, including grammar, punctuation, spelling, and the formal elements of visual texts. This knowledge is essential for responding to, discussing, critiquing, editing, and revising print and nonprint texts.

Writers move fluidly from whole to part and back again, shaping and defining their overall purpose as they develop specific examples and refine passages. They are problem-solvers, deciding as they go along how to tackle the many different challenges that arise.

Students develop their knowledge of form and convention in spoken, written, and visual language as they create their own compositions and critique those of others. Whether they are just learning to orchestrate text in a left-to-right direction across a blank page, matching letters to the sounds they hear in words they want to spell, varying their range of sentence structure in a written piece, or experimenting with the arrangement and balance of visual elements in an illustration, students need to understand that attention to structure and form is an essential part of the process of creating and revising text. Students who can draw on a deep knowledge of language structure find that the texts they create are both more accessible and more effective for their various audiences.

Spoken, visual, and written composition alike require the ability to grasp whole-to-part relationships. Students who work with films, for example, become aware of editing strategies that are used to weave together individual scenes in order to produce a continuous narrative. The careful study of illustrations—whether in children's stories or individual artworks—helps build knowledge of formal characteristics such as balance, composition, unity, and symmetry (or asymmetry). An exploration of color, interestingly, may be connected to notions such as mood or tone in written and performance works. A seventh-grade teacher in Philadelphia, for example, asks his students to depict the moods evoked in Madeleine L'Engle's *A Wrinkle in Time* by cutting colored paper into shapes that seem to convey the tone of the chapter, then explaining their artistic depictions. Students who explore such cross-disciplinary connections as they develop a working terminology to describe language structure become more thorough readers and more effective writers.

As their peers respond to their compositions, students often discover that they need explicit instruction in particular aspects of writing or editing. A student may recognize, for instance, that readers are baffled by his or her use of conflicting metaphors in a paragraph, or are confused about when sentence fragments are acceptable in written texts. Or a student may wish to explore ways to use punctuation more effectively in order to develop more complex, varied sentence patterns in his or her prose. Explicit instruction on such topics is most likely to be effective when it is offered in the context of real writing and peer-editing activities. Research has shown convincingly that neither isolated exercises nor the study of formal systems of grammar independent of context affects most students' actual speaking and writing skills.

By closely observing students' writing processes and carefully reading their work, teachers can see which aspects of language structure are giving students trouble and help them learn these concepts through direct instruction and practice. It is also important for students to discover that grammar, spelling, and punctuation are useful not only in the context of fixing problems or mistakes; they can be studied effectively in a workshop context in which students work together to expand their repertoire of syntactic and verbal styles. When students connect the study of grammar and language patterns to the wider purposes of communication and artistic development, they are considerably more likely to incorporate such study into their working knowledge.

Indeed, through their writing, editing, and revising experiences, students come to understand that a composition may never be truly finished. Although a paper may be turned in, or a performance completed, we can always rethink, rework, and refine. The ability to step back and critique our work with an eye to improving it is essential to good writing and to both spoken and graphic compositions. As the term *revision* suggests, we can always see our work again differently, or through the eyes of another reader or another writer. Students who understand this are better able to strengthen their competencies as writers.

Critique and revision—seeing again, differently—are crucial not only for students in the process of developing their skills as, say, storytellers or playwrights; they are also essential for a deeper understanding of our culture. That is, students' ability to critique and respond meaningfully to peers' written and spoken texts relates in important ways to their ability to "read" culture and society from an informed, thoughtful perspective. For example, by studying the structure of narrative in film—analyzing elements such as framing, shot selection, and the use of voice-over and dialogue—students become more adept and perceptive viewers of television commercials, news, and drama.

7 *Students conduct research on issues and interests by generating ideas and questions, and by posing problems. They gather, evaluate, and synthesize data from a variety of sources (e.g., print and nonprint texts, artifacts, people) to communicate their discoveries in ways that suit their purpose and audience.*

The ability to generate questions, identify issues, pose problems, and seek out answers is at the core of productive human living. In some measure, we engage in research whenever we reflect on our problems and concerns, even when our hypotheses are limited in number or sophistication. Our curiosity often inspires us to focus on solving problems and investigating issues. From a very early age, we try to make sense of our physical world and the world of ideas that surrounds us.

It is essential that students acquire a wide range of abilities and tools for raising questions, investigating concerns, and solving problems. In school, "research" is the name commonly given to the processes of addressing such concerns. However, a rigid view of research as a series of mechanical steps misrepresents the complexity and creative potential of human problem solving and limits the range of educational experiences that can help students. Perhaps the idea of research is best considered in terms of inquiry—the learner's desire to look deeply into a question or idea that interests him or her. Viewed in this way, research becomes an investigation into an issue or problem chosen by the student. It involves posing interesting and substantive questions, identifying and securing multiple data sources, analyzing and synthesizing data, and positing findings or new understandings.

Language itself is a valuable research tool. The ability to use language to seek out and refine interesting questions, plan, predict, investigate, analyze, hypothesize, and speculate gives students a way to frame and address the issues that they encounter in academic subjects as well as in everyday life. Students often use language to investigate questions and tackle prob-

I believe that every child begins with the drive to explore the world he [or she] is born into, that curiosity is indeed "native." Speech becomes its principal instrument.

—James Britton

lems, but these experiences are frequently overlooked simply because they are so common. The application of spoken language to problem solving is especially pervasive. Students are constantly using talk informally, to negotiate among themselves and with others and to express their ideas about school problems and social dilemmas.

Everyday life provides abundant raw materials from which students can develop their investigative language competencies. For example, a class of middle school students in Iowa were concerned with a local crime problem and decided to do something about it. These students began their investigation by discussing the problem with people in their community. These discussions helped the students to narrow the focus of their inquiry and to identify key people who could talk to the entire class about particular criminal acts or issues. The students also gathered statistical and other data from appropriate sources, read books on crime, and clipped and shared articles from various periodicals. Once the students had gathered the information they found necessary, they analyzed it and formulated courses of action. Some students wrote letters to the local newspaper; others wrote to the chief of police to offer solutions that they thought would reduce the crime rate. Still others prepared oral presentations to share with elementary school students, alerting them to criminal acts that could affect them. The students involved in this project used their language and research skills to confront real issues in their community.

Students need to learn creative and multifaceted approaches to research and inquiry. The ability to identify good topics, to gather information, and to evaluate, assemble, and interpret findings from among the many general and specialized information sources now available to them is one of the most vital skills that students can acquire.

8 *Students use a variety of technological and informational resources (e.g., libraries, databases, computer networks, video) to gather and synthesize information and to create and communicate knowledge.*

To take advantage of the resources that technology offers and to become prepared for the demands that will face them in the future, students need to learn how to use an array of technologies, from computers and computer networks to electronic mail, interactive video, and CD-ROMs. Technology opens up new worlds to students, making available a tremendous assortment of information, ideas, and images. It also provides new motivation for writing and allows students to assume greater responsibility for their own learning. For example, students are stimulated by the relative ease and flexibility of revising and

editing online and by the prospect of printing and circulating their writings. Indeed, even very young students like to compose on the computer. Teachers can build on these interests by acting as guides and observers, facilitating learning and helping students discover, evaluate, and mine the many resources available to them.

Students should use computers, then, to compose texts and graphics for themselves and others and to publish their own works. This requires skill in keyboarding and word processing as students draft, revise, and edit their writings, seeking feedback from peers and teachers along the way. Students should use computers individually and collaboratively to develop and publish a variety of works such as storybooks, essays, newsletters, classroom anthologies, and school newspapers. Also, extended use of computers should be encouraged when connection to a network makes it possible to correspond with others nearby or far away.

A creative and empowering use of recent technology is demonstrated in the following classroom example. Video-recording helped fifth- and sixth-grade students in an urban Phoenix school to communicate with a group of pen pals from a Navajo reservation in rural Arizona. The Phoenix students videotaped their homes (in public housing projects), as well as their school and playground, using both words and images to describe for their Navajo friends where they lived and what their daily lives were like. The Navajo students responded with their own videotapes, forming a multimedia correspondence which helped both groups better understand life for someone else of the same age in a different geographic and cultural setting. The two groups of students not only learned about life elsewhere, but also gained experience in using video technology to represent themselves to others. Along the way, they saw the power of visual representation and its importance in enriching a sense of cultural identity.

Students need to use new technologies to gain access to databases, bibliographies, other data resources, and computer users around the world, and they need to develop skill in synthesizing this broad base of information. Student inquiry, problem solving, and formal research at all levels are taking on a new character. A generation ago, students were generally limited to seeking out resource materials for traditional research papers in library card catalogs and standard encyclopedias and reference sources. They now have a wealth of resources, the very abundance and complexity of which require new levels of sophistication in search techniques and an expanded ability to choose, assess, and synthesize materials. Direct instruction in electronic resources is becoming increasingly important in today's classrooms.

Many teachers are not yet comfortable with new technologies, however, and require professional development opportunities in order to meet the technological needs of their students. On the positive side, teachers can often be co-learners with their students, many of whom are more familiar with computer jargon, the Internet, search techniques, and available resources. Teachers should welcome this activity, giving students the enjoyment and pride of sometimes being their teachers' teachers.

Electronic technologies, perhaps more than any other recent innovation, have heightened our sense of the need for reform and have raised our expectations of what students must know and be able to do in English language arts. It is therefore crucial that we address the uneven distribution of technology in our nation's schools. Some schools have abundant computers for students to use, while others have only a few, which are often reserved for the students regarded as academically advanced. Students in economically disadvantaged communities and those labeled as less proficient often lack access to new technologies or are confined to routine computer activities that fail to challenge and develop their minds. Schools and communities need to address these inequities to ensure that all students can become technologically literate.

9 Students develop an understanding of and respect for diversity in language use, patterns, and dialects across cultures, ethnic groups, geographic regions, and social roles.

The capacity to hear and respect different perspectives and to communicate with people whose lives and cultures are different from our own is a vital element of American society. Language is a powerful medium through which we develop social and cultural understanding, and the need to foster this understanding is growing increasingly urgent as our culture becomes more diverse. Students deserve and need learning environments that respect cultural, racial, and ethnic differences. Celebrating our shared beliefs and traditions is not enough; we also need to honor that which is distinctive in the many groups that make up our nation.

Students who have difficulty relating to peers from different cultures may find it easier to understand their classmates' unfamiliar backgrounds and experiences—and may discover unexpected similarities—when they read and discuss stories and other texts that dramatize cultural frameworks and relationships. By understanding and appreciating differences, students build the groundwork for unity and shared experience. One way of approaching this is seen in a culturally diverse classroom in the Bronx. Students in language arts classes there select literary works that explore their specific cultural and ethnic backgrounds. In addition to discussing these works as a group, the students write book reviews that are collected in a booklet distributed to the entire class and placed in the school library. This student-directed work encourages children and young adults to study both their own backgrounds and those of others in their school community.

Students bring into the language arts classroom not only values and beliefs but also ways of seeing the world. Ethnicity and culture go beyond visible markers of difference (such as speech, dress, interpersonal styles, food) to encompass larger issues of perception and interpretation. Students who explore linguistic diversity among their peers discover that language use, dialect, and accent are cues for other kinds of differences, and investigating these language features thoughtfully allows the discovery that different cultures' diverse ways of knowing the world are embodied in their languages. In this way, the study of language diversity opens onto subjects such as history, science, and social studies. Students can explore, for instance, the history of oral cultures and their many philosophical and

Celebrating our shared beliefs and traditions is not enough; we also need to honor that which is distinctive in the many groups that make up our nation.

religious traditions, or the importance of nonwestern cultures in the development of mathematics.

Schools are responsible for creating a climate of respect for the variety of languages that students speak and the variety of cultures from which they come. Students as well as teachers need to recognize and appreciate linguistic and cultural variation, for it is truly an asset, not a liability. Students from a variety of backgrounds can connect their in- and out-of-school experiences in meaningful ways. They should address questions such as these: What beliefs and traditions are important to me and to other students? What connections can we trace across our backgrounds? What values are shared among the various cultures we represent? How do we view the world from different perspectives? Awareness of the connections between language and culture, and exposure to variations in language use, are important dimensions of teaching and learning in the English language arts.

Students need opportunities to recognize and honor cultural differences in ways that extend beyond the ability to adapt to and communicate in a multicultural society. Recognizing that ethnic or racial bias is often embedded in language or metaphor, for example, may lead students to a deeper understanding of the power of figurative language to shape perception. Similarly, students who trace the evolution of various dialects and speech patterns can learn about the interconnectedness of language and social history. Knowing how to share and construct meaning with peers across racial and cultural boundaries enables all students to appreciate the richness and power of language.

Knowing how to share and construct meaning with peers across racial and cultural boundaries enables all students to appreciate the richness and power of language.

10 *Students whose first language is not English make use of their first language to develop competency in the English language arts and to develop understanding of content across the curriculum.*

Linguistic diversity is becoming more common in our nation's classrooms, as growing numbers of students have primary languages that are not English. Accordingly, there is increasing debate as to how schools should develop these students' academic competencies and their English language proficiency.

Students whose first language is not English are more likely to achieve academic success in English in settings where their primary language is nurtured. This position is affirmed by current research on language learning. Contrary to popular misconceptions, school-age children do not necessarily learn a second language quickly and easily. The development of competency in English is most effective when students are in programs that build on their first language. The use of primary language in the curriculum provides a support system for learning English, for making learning in other subject areas more comprehensible, and for helping students to gain confidence both socially and academically.

Thus, there is an urgent need for programs that enable students who speak other languages to attain proficiency in English while at the same time providing them the support they need to continue developing competency in their first language. Programs of this nature, of course, are not always possible. In some schools, for example, the number of students who speak a particular language is too small to entitle the school under current federal or state regulations to fund a bilingual program. In such cases, students typically learn English in an English as a Second Language (ESL) program. Even under these circumstances, however, schools can offer students support in their primary language by seeking out other adults (including parents) or students who speak the language in order to help translate or clarify concepts.

It is important to bear in mind that even bilingual students who are confident and proficient speakers of English often have difficulty grasping the specialized concepts in other subject areas. If support in their first language is withdrawn too early, they are placed at a disadvantage in schooling. Whenever possible, then, students whose first language is not English should learn and study content in their first language while learning English as a second language. Eventually, as their English proficiency develops, they can move into content area classes conducted in English. Of course, students benefit when they can continue studying content in both languages.

On the other hand, it is vitally important that students whose primary language is not English be included as fully as possible in the mainstream of school activities. Providing support in their first language must not result in their separation or segregation from English-language speakers. Social interaction is essential for language learning, and it is vitally important that all students who are learning English be provided with ample opportunities for developing their English through conversations with others.

Furthermore, we must recognize that learning English as a second, or third, or fourth language is a challenging and complex process, and our response to the needs of students who are developing proficiency in English must do justice to these complexities. Rather than generalizing about children who are learning English as a second language, we must remember how students may differ. For example, some older students who are learning English have already devel-

oped proficiency in both academic and conversational use of their native language, while others may be proficient in their native everyday language but have limited academic language skills.

The language capabilities and challenges facing every child, including those who are learning English as a second language, must be carefully considered as we plan experiences and instruction.

11 Students participate as knowledgeable, reflective, creative, and critical members of a variety of literacy communities.

Members of any literacy community share interests in certain kinds of texts and have similar ways of talking about and responding to those texts and the issues they raise. Students belong to many different communities of language users—communities that include their peers, teachers, friends, and family members. Students also participate in other, more dispersed literacy communities, comprising, say, readers of a popular genre, like science fiction, or viewers of Hitchcock films. In any community—and literacy communities are no exception—each individual assumes a role, and these roles evolve as the members of the community spend time together.

Students should develop an awareness of their own participation in various literacy communities and their roles within them. Students are likely to identify some of their literacy communities quite readily: if they participate in an online discussion group on rainforest conservation, for example, they have already made conscious choices to identify with that language group and to share their thoughts with members of that group via computer network. Other literacy communities, though, may be less immediately apparent. Peer and cultural communities, for example, exert a powerful although sometimes subtle influence on students' language. Connecting their experiences in these communities with their in-school study of language strengthens students' competency as language users and their awareness of the power and versatility of literacy.

Goals lack meaning if students are not motivated to integrate their knowledge willingly, effectively, and joyfully into their lives outside the classroom.

By developing awareness of their own roles within different literacy communities, students can see how language usage varies across different contexts and audiences. Much like language conventions, literacy communities emerge within a social context which may be geographically defined, or, as in the case of many online communities, widely dispersed. As students discover their connections to such communities, they learn to think of themselves as knowledgeable participants in the process of using language to share ideas.

Students not only join existing literacy communities, they also create them. A student telling his or her friends or classmates a story, for example, is creating a community of engaged listeners by building their interest in the characters and events of the narrative. A group of students working together on a research project develop a community of shared interests and common questions as they investigate a problem and compile information resources on their chosen subject.

In the literacy community of the classroom, students' work merits serious attention by peers and teacher alike. As community members, students use language in a variety of ways. For example, they may read and respond to one another's writing. They may listen to one another read aloud, cri-

Standards for the English Language Arts

tiquing the performance for fluency and effectiveness, or sharing their personal responses to an author's work. Or they may work together in a group to solve a persistent problem in their school, e.g., "How can we convince the principal to buy bike racks for the school?" In each case, students and teachers are there for one another, benefiting from one another's insights and knowledge.

Students who work with one another as authors and readers of texts discover the many ways in which a given text can be interpreted and the many ways in which their personal experiences and knowledge influence the construction of meanings. By reading what others write, and listening to what they say, students have a window into lives beyond their own. Teachers who recognize the value of literacy communities will make sure that students have opportunities to work together and that students have the skills they need to be supportive and productive members of these communities.

The concept of the literacy community emphasizes the collaborative nature of much language learning. Whether students' participation in a given community is face-to-face (as in the case of friends and classmates) or technologically mediated (as in the case of popular media and computer networking), it is an essential part of their coming to view themselves as effective language users.

12 *Students use spoken, written, and visual language to accomplish their own purposes (e.g., for learning, enjoyment, persuasion, and the exchange of information).*

The work of the school must have an effect on the language and literacy choices made by individual students outside of the classroom—both in the present and into their post-school lives. Performing various class assignments and meeting these content standards are essential, but ultimately these goals lack meaning if students are not motivated to integrate their knowledge willingly, effectively, and joyfully into their lives outside the classroom.

Of course, many of these standards emphasize links between in-school and out-of-school experiences. They focus, for example, on relationships between home language and school language; on wide-ranging audiences for students' writings; on variations in language use according to different social environments; on everyday applications of school learning; on technological and community resources that extend the boundaries of learning; and on connecting the student with diverse cultures in the school, the community, the nation, and the world. Students must also choose to make those linkages work in their own lives, however.

This final standard is clearly related to the ideal of producing lifelong learners—a goal that goes beyond the school years. It is true that we cannot be certain in the present moment that we are helping to shape the well-motivated adult who is committed to continuing self-education. Nevertheless, we can create the conditions that are likely to lead to lifelong learning, and this objective must be central if schooling is to be meaningful and not merely a forced march through academic exercises.

There are, in fact, clear signs during the school years which indicate that students are developing strong learning habits in and positive attitudes

At school my teachers were listening to me stumble through the Dick and Jane readers. They would have been amazed to know about my secret life in which I was feasting on great fat books with many-syllabled words I've never learned how to pronounce properly.

—Katherine Paterson, "The Secret Life of Katherine Clements Womeldorf," *Once Upon a Time . . .*

toward the English language arts. Students may, for example, independently decide to read more books by authors they have studied or on themes they have discussed in class. They may talk in the cafeteria or after school about issues and questions that were raised in the classroom. They may express their views thoughtfully and respect others' perspectives, as modeled in good classroom interaction. They may mention, perhaps during class discussion or in their journals, works they have composed on their own, such as poems, diaries, family letters, e-mail exchanges, petitions, or home video productions. Their parents may notice student choices that appear to be influenced by the school's English language arts program, perhaps commenting on more leisure reading or on more selective reading and television viewing.

Students' self-motivation, then, is not merely a wish for the future. It is a pervasive concern, evident in both subtle and more obvious ways in students' lives within and beyond the classroom.

REALIZING THE STANDARDS

Imagine a classroom in which all of these standards are realized, in which the goals we have articulated and discussed here form the daily foundation of English language arts experiences. Students are engaged in small-group and individual research projects that link classroom and academic inquiry to their lived social and family experiences. They tell each other stories, argue constructively, share resources, read newspaper articles aloud to one another, make collages and videotapes, and write letters and essays. Displays of students' writing and graphics welcome visitors to the classroom and enhance students' sense of being part of a vital language community both within and beyond the school.

This kind of classroom, idealized as it may sound, can be and is being realized across the land every day. The standards listed here are a way of highlighting these practices and articulating the consensus already being developed among teachers around the country who are bringing out the best in their students day by day.

CHAPTER 4 STANDARDS IN THE CLASSROOM

Decisions about how the English language arts standards will be realized in particular classrooms need to be made locally. As we have affirmed throughout this document, it is the individuals working directly with students who are best equipped to make the judgments and commitments needed to bring the standards to life. Only when students, parents, and communities discuss their vision of language arts education, when administrators work to make the most of their schools' resources, and when teachers attend to their students' particular strengths and needs can these standards be realized.

This chapter offers some perspective on how the standards might be implemented by looking at a selection of classroom vignettes. Students in these classrooms are engaged in challenging, purposeful language experiences that draw on and enhance their competencies in all six of the language arts. These experiences help them gain the knowledge, confidence, and creativity to be fully literate participants in their world. Like the brief examples of classroom practice offered elsewhere in this document, these vignettes are presented as further reflections on the standards, not as models that embody their thorough realization. Although the approaches to teaching and learning depicted in the vignettes are in general positive examples, they are intended to encourage critical review and discussion among teachers and other readers of this document.

The vignettes are not meant to correlate directly with individual standards; in fact, each depicts a rich learning experience that incorporates several standards simultaneously. These examples of classroom practice make clear the important interrelations among the different language arts, as among the standards themselves. In so doing, they highlight both the complexities and the serendipities of literacy learning.

Between five and seven vignettes are presented for each level of schooling: elementary, middle, and secondary.[1] Although the grade levels are typically indicated in each classroom example, the learning and teaching events presented are relevant and applicable for students at other levels as well. We therefore encourage teachers to read through all of these classroom portraits and not to limit themselves to the selections from their own teaching levels.

---

1. The vignettes are drawn from actual classrooms and depict real classroom practices; however, some details have been recast slightly to emphasize particular aspects of the standards.

Each vignette is followed by two or three questions that frame the learning experiences depicted from a wider perspective. Characteristically, these questions focus on alternatives that might be considered in the activities presented, issues not fully addressed, and possible adaptations of the insights reflected in the classroom samples. The questions posed in these sections, like the vignettes themselves, invite readers to participate in an ongoing conversation about classroom practices. We encourage readers to use the questions to consider the vignettes' applicability in their own curricula and as a starting point for discussion among colleagues.

ELEMENTARY VIGNETTES

Elementary Vignette 1

Twenty-six first graders in an urban Philadelphia school crowd around their teacher as she pulls a new picture book out of her tote bag. She places the book on her lap, quietly signaling the students to find a place to sit on the rug and get ready to share a very special story.

Once the children settle down, the teacher holds up *Snowballs*, by Lois Ehlert, and she and the children laugh and talk about the picture on the cover, which shows a snowman with a bird on his head. Before opening the book, the teacher asks the students if anyone can read the title. Lauren replies by sounding out /sn/ and then saying, "Snowman." The teacher tells Lauren that she used some good strategies to read the title; she used her knowledge of the sounds of the beginning letters along with the clues from the picture on the cover. Then the teacher covers the word *snow* and asks Lauren to look carefully at the word *balls*. Lauren sounds out /b/ and scans to the end of the word before saying, "Snowball. Oh, it says snowballs." The teacher reminds Lauren to be sure to look at the middle and end of a word, as well as the beginning, to gather clues to what the word says and means.

Ravi joins the discussion and says he figured out the title by looking at the two words: *snow* and *balls*. The teacher tells the class that Ravi has just given them yet another way to recognize a word. She then quickly reviews the three word-recognition strategies Lauren and Ravi used to figure out the title of the book: looking at and sounding out the letters at the beginning, middle, and end of a word; looking at the picture; and looking for known words within a larger, unfamiliar word. She tells them that after story time, she will add these strategies to their class chart titled "Strategies We Use to Understand What We Read." She also makes a mental note to introduce compound words to the class at another time, using Ravi's example to demonstrate how compound words are formed and how that knowledge can be used to decode words.

After this brief discussion about the title, the teacher asks the students if they have any idea how snowballs might be important to the story, and if they can predict what will happen in the story. Alex suggests that the characters will make a snowman or a snow fort and that it will melt. The students then listen intently as the teacher reads the first few pages of the story. The teacher pauses briefly to discuss the prediction Alex made and to see if he wants to revise his prediction. She then continues reading the story of a child who spends a glorious snowball day creating a snow family, including a snow dad, a snow mom, a snow boy, a snow girl, a snow baby, and a snow cat and dog. Unfortunately, when the sun comes out, the child has to watch each member of the snow family slowly melt away. This story, of course, elicits more talk among the teacher and students about their own wonderful "snowball days."

- How important is a noncompetitive, risk-taking environment to the learning process?
- How might the teacher keep track of student strengths and needs observed during whole-class discussions, so that she can use this knowledge to support students during individual reading conferences?

Elementary Vignette 2

Maya and Katherine are students in a multiage class (6-, 7-, and 8-year-olds) in a small rural elementary school. Recently, the two of them collaborated to write a fable entitled "Frown and Smiles," which featured a rabbit and a chipmunk as the main characters. In the fable, Maya and Katherine have their characters argue, then walk off in different directions toward their homes. Before they reach their homes, however, the rabbit and the chipmunk bump headlong into each other.

During class sharing time, the girls read a draft of their fable to the entire class. Their classmates like the story but wonder how the animals could bump into each other if they walked off in different directions. Maya and Katherine try to explain how this might occur, but they fail to help the class (and even each other) understand. The two girls realize that they have a problem to solve if they want to keep this part in their story, so they use their writing time to role-play the two characters walking off in different directions and bumping into one another. After much rehearsal and discussion, they figure out that if the rabbit and chipmunk walk off in different directions but follow the same circular route, they will eventually end up in the same place. When the teacher checks on the progress of their revision, Maya and Katherine explain their discovery and their plan to have the animals take a circular route rather than a straight one. The teacher points out, however, that two characters with presumably good eyesight would probably see each other coming. Maya and Katherine ponder this comment.

The next day during class sharing time, the girls present their new version of the story, which details the rabbit and the chipmunk walking off in different directions but on the same circular path, while looking down at their feet as they walk because they are angry. Maya and Katherine then show their classmates their latest plan: a rough sketch of an illustrated map that shows the circular route, the characters' homes, and the two characters bumping heads. The girls' classmates applaud the changes to the story and are especially impressed with the addition of the illustrated map. Several children comment that a map might be a good idea for the stories they are working on. After sharing time, Maya and Katherine rush off to work on their map and produce a final draft of their fable.

- How effective is drama as a revision process? What other processes besides rewriting and drama might students use to make sense of their work?
- How does this class's literacy community function to serve these young writers?
- What types of instruction and guidance must this teacher have provided to get a group of students to achieve this level of independence?

Elementary Vignette 3

Pollution in the water supply has become a topic of widespread discussion in one Northeastern town. After an order to boil public water is issued and is covered extensively by the local media, a group of fifth graders takes an interest in water purification. Four students—Tomas, Liz, Harrison, and Cecilia—decide to make water purification the subject of their inquiry project and to prepare a presentation for the class. They name themselves the Water Purification Team.

The four students spend a day reading different sources and talking among themselves to define the questions they will need to explore in more detail. After an initial conference with their teacher about which resources would be most useful, the students decide to begin their search with the newspaper, and to seek out local sources of information. Working with the school librarian, Liz and Harrison uncover information that extends well beyond the encyclopedia, which had been the starting point for their research. A database search shows the availability of numerous books, films, free pamphlets, magazine articles, and other materials. Cecilia and Tomas call the water company and talk to a spokesperson there. They also speak with a reporter who has written several articles on water supply problems for the local newspaper.

The students' research expands to include taped interviews with the water company representative and the reporter and a tour of the water plant. After reviewing all of the material gathered in their research, the students work together to outline their presentations. They divide their presentation into three parts: a description of how water purification works, using charts they drew; an explanation of how an aging piping system is causing the problems in the town's water supply; and a mini-debate between Cecilia and Tomas about whether a new piping system should be funded by raising the cost of the water or by new taxes (an issue that had been raised, but not resolved, by the newspaper reporter). The presentation generates enthusiastic responses and many questions from their classmates, and the Water Purification Team considers its project a major success.

- In what ways was this research project an instance of integrated language arts and interdisciplinary activity?
- What are the benefits of this type of activity for both younger and older students?
- How can a teacher adapt a planned curriculum to allow students to take up interests that emerge, as in this example?

Elementary Vignette 4

Keoni is a kindergarten student of Native Hawaiian ancestry whose primary language is Hawaiian Creole English, a nonmainstream variety of English which most people in Hawaii refer to as "pidgin." Keoni has learned many Hawaiian words from his family, although he does not speak the Hawaiian language.

When Keoni entered kindergarten, his teacher noticed that he could tell many stories, especially about camping at the beach with his family. He did not have books at home, and his first exposure to the language of books occurred in the classroom. Keoni's teacher read to her students every day, exposing them to an array of picture books and informational books in large and regular formats. She also took dictation from the students, transcribing their words onto chart paper and encouraging them to share their ideas and stories with one another. Through these activities, the students learned important concepts about print and about oral language. As Keoni watched and listened to the teacher reading and pointing to the words in books and on the charts, he began to notice patterns in the language. He added his voice on familiar refrains, and he began to attend to the print on the page, noticing words and letters.

During story reading one morning, the teacher read a fable about a coyote and a flock of crows. The fable included the words *roaches* and *crows*. Some of the children seemed puzzled by these words, so the teacher pointed to the illustrations and asked if the children knew what these animals were. Several children used the terms "cock-a-roach" and "mynah bird." The teacher praised the children for these observations. She pointed out that *roach* was another word for "cock-a-roach" and explained that while crows were noisy like mynah birds, they were larger and were not found in Hawaii.

When the teacher finished reading the story, Keoni eagerly joined in the discussion. He stated that the coyote was a *niele* (nee-eh´-lay)—the Hawaiian word for a nosy creature. His teacher and several of the students laughed appreciatively at the connection Keoni had made between his home language and the events in the story. "Yes," she said, "the coyote is a *niele*, or you could say he is nosy or curious."

Near the end of the discussion, the teacher shifted the students' attention from the content of the story to the structures of particular words. She wrote the words *coyote*, *roach*, and *crow* on the chalkboard and asked for volunteers to mark what they noticed about the words. Keoni raised his hand, and when he went to the chalkboard, he circled the *C*s at the beginning of *coyote* and *crow*. "Like Candy," he said, referring to the name of one of his classmates. The teacher praised Keoni and said that yes, both words began with the letter *C*, which was also the first letter in Candy's name, and that *Candy, coyote,* and *crow* all began with the same *sound* as well.

- What benefits do students gain from having their home language validated and used as a curricular resource?

- How do the underlying assumptions about emergent literacy fit with your own or your district's curriculum? If they are consistent with your beliefs about teaching and learning, but not with your district's, how might you get your district to learn about them?

- In what ways can the concept of emergent literacy be a useful reference for understanding the literacy development of older students as well as those just starting school?

Elementary Vignette 5

Katelyn, a third-grade student, has just returned to school after spending several days at home with strep throat. During writers' workshop, she decides to write a Mother's Day letter thanking her mother for the good care she gave her while she was sick. Mr. J., the teacher, observes Katelyn as she sits and thinks about what to write. She sits quietly for several minutes, not writing anything, and then suddenly her pencil seems to fly across the page as she writes:

> Dear mom,
> Happy Mothers day mom. I like when your are funny. I like you when you are happy! I think of you every day. Your so clever your so kind you'll never never leave my mind. Rember when I had strep thort I thought I had a frog in my thorot. Rember when you made me a milkshake when I had strep throt was that milkshake ever tasty. Goodbye Goodbye I half to go goodbye goodbye I love you so!
>
> LOVE,
> Katelyn

Jia-Ling, who sits next to Katelyn, asks her what she is writing, so Katelyn reads her the letter. Jia-Ling says it sounds like a poem, and they both laugh. Then Sarah and Kyle join them. Sarah says her mom fixes her milkshakes, too, when she is sick. They all agree that milkshakes are their favorite kind of medicine. When Mr. J. stops by Katelyn's table, he asks the students what they are discussing, and Katelyn explains that they are talking about the letter she is writing to her mom and that Jia-Ling thinks it sounds like a poem. Mr. J. reads the letter and says he agrees with Jia-Ling. He asks Katelyn if she has considered turning the letter into a poem. Katelyn says she thought about it, but she likes her letter the way it is. She then asks Mr. J. if he will help her fix her spelling.

- What instructional strategies might help Katelyn to understand that revising writing is more than adding a few details to a piece or correcting the spelling?

- What does Katelyn know about the function of exclamation points and hyphens? How can Mr. J. use what she knows to extend her understanding?

Elementary Vignette 6

Students in a fourth-grade classroom read independently each day while their teacher confers with individual students. For the past three weeks, Mike has begun the independent reading period with the same complaint: "I can't read. I hate to read. There's no good books out there. Well, there are no good books I can read!" On this particular day, the teacher notes Mike's behavior and writes "Book Selection Conference" by his name on her planning schedule.

At the beginning of the conference, the teacher tells Mike that she has some ideas about books he might like to read and suggests that they visit the classroom library area. Knowing Mike's interest in sports, the teacher pulls out a copy of *Skinnybones* by Barbara Park. "Mike, you're on a baseball team, and you have a good sense of humor. Somehow this book reminds me of you." They spend a few minutes together, the teacher reading aloud and Mike listening. When she reads the part about Skinnybones wanting to fit into a size large baseball shirt, he laughs. Next, the teacher flips to her son's favorite section, where Skinnybones gets a buzz haircut, and invites Mike to read that section to her. He reluctantly takes the book and begins to read. Within a minute he is laughing again. The teacher asks if he would like to give *Skinnybones* a try. He takes the book and walks toward his desk. The teacher says she will check back with him shortly as she calls another student to join her for a conference.

Mike does read *Skinnybones*, and then he reads *Almost Starring Skinnybones*. In his literature log, he writes that he preferred the first book because ". . . it was just funnier, but I really like the way the author makes characters like real kids."

Postscript: This incident occurred when Mike was in fourth grade. When he was in seventh grade, he stopped by to visit his fourth-grade teacher. As he entered the room, the first thing he said was: "Hey, Miss J., remember that day we read Skinnybones?"

- In what ways has the teacher demonstrated her knowledge of both child development and the content of English language arts instruction?

- What are some ways in which teachers and parents can help reluctant readers to develop an interest in reading for pleasure?

- How do teachers decide when to let students choose their own reading material and when to choose for them?

Elementary Vignette 7

Mrs. D., a teacher in the upper elementary grades, is conducting a mini-lesson on reading strategies. She tells the students that she often stops her reading at particular points in a story to picture scenes or characters in her head. She explains that this helps her understand the characters and gives her a better sense of the place and time of the story. At the end of the lesson, Mrs. D. invites her students to try this strategy as they read a book of their own choosing. After spending a few minutes circulating and checking with students during this silent reading period, the teacher also reads. The class is completely quiet, except for the sound of pages turning, as the students and teacher read independently.

Eight minutes before the end of the class period, the students gather for a sharing time. The teacher begins, as she always does, by asking, "How did it go today?"

Marco speaks first. "I tried to see the story in my head, kind of like it was a movie, and I found myself getting more interested in what I was reading. Yesterday I had trouble understanding this story [*Hatchet*, by Gary Paulsen], but today when I tried to see it in my head, it made more sense. I saw Brian hitting the hatchet against the rock and I saw the sparks, too. Seeing it like a movie in my head really helped me understand what I was reading."

Jennifer offers her perspective next. "I tried this strategy, but it didn't work as good for me. I like pretending to be the character better. Pretending I'm the character really helps me understand what I read. I did see some of the story in my head, but it was like I was looking through Cleo's [the protagonist of *The Island Keeper*, by Harry Mazer] eyes instead of seeing a movie. I think that's different from what Marco did, but that's what worked for me."

The teacher invites further comments.

"I read both those books," Brandy says, "and I think I used Jen's strategy for both. Actually, I think I usually use both of those strategies, but sometimes one is stronger and sometimes the other is stronger."

The teacher explains that Brandy probably did use both strategies. One strategy does *not* work in every situation, she points out to the class; readers need to make flexible use of a range of strategies.

- How does discussion about reading strategies help students gain greater competence and independence as readers?

- What should a teacher do for students who over-rely on one strategy?

MIDDLE SCHOOL VIGNETTES

Middle School Vignette 1

A class of eighth-grade students in Tennessee is introduced to young adult literature when their teacher brings a cart loaded with more than 100 young adult titles into their classroom. They watch and listen as the teacher reads selected passages, describes several of the books' plots, and recruits students to help dramatize a few important scenes. After this formal introduction, the students select several books that capture their attention. They browse through them independently for a while as their teacher posts on the bulletin board summaries and reviews written by previous students. Each student decides on a book to read, and students form small groups with peers interested in the same books or books by the same author.

Jessie, Joanna, and Kelsie, who often work together, become reading partners. Joanna, who has recently lost an older sister in a car accident, selects *My Daniel* by Pam Conrad, a novel about a young girl whose brother dies. Her reading partners also select books by Conrad, with Jessie choosing *Taking the Ferry Home* and Kelsie selecting *Holding Me Here*. As the three students read, they hold personal conferences and use journals to share episodes with one another; sometimes they exchange books to share excerpts that are especially relevant to their own lives. Other students occasionally join the group's conversation and discuss questions that help them to understand and cope with the death of Joanna's sister.

Janice, intrigued by what she hears about S. E. Hinton, chooses *Taming the Star Runner*, *The Outsiders*, and *Tex*. She tells her reading partners that she picked these titles because Hinton's books deal with young boys who are fatherless, and that she identifies strongly with those characters. In later conversations, Janice explains that she is without parents because her father is in jail awaiting trial for killing her mother. Many students are startled and confused by this news, but others go on to talk about characters in books they are reading who had also lost family members.

As the students become more familiar with particular authors, they present the books they have been reading to their classmates through dramatic booktalks (modeled on their teacher's presentation the first day), visual presentations, and oral readings. The students also write response essays/reviews for one another, explaining why they liked a book or series of books by an author and encouraging their classmates to read them as well. These responses will be saved so that next year's students can read how their peers responded to works that helped them understand their own lives more clearly.

- How important to the curriculum is knowing the students' lives outside of the classroom? What activities can be used to get to know students better?
- How do these types of interactions and personal responses help students to become more competent and critical readers and thinkers?

Middle School Vignette 2

A group of sixth-grade students is reading and studying science texts, such as primary sources, magazine articles, textbooks, and essays on scientific and environmental topics. As part of a thematic exploration of large mammals, the students read a number of magazine articles on endangered animals and work in small groups to practice using study strategies such as underlining, annotating, and summarizing information through visual diagrams. Their teacher models study strategies in explicit class demonstrations.

One day, before reading an article on grizzly bears, the students talk about specific ways of learning and remembering important ideas and information encountered during reading. The teacher models strategies she uses as she reads, such as underlining and note taking, "thinking aloud" for the class as she sifts through information to highlight and organize important points. She shows students a way in which to transform key ideas and details that support them into a

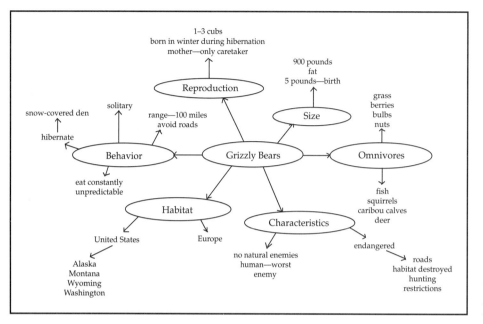

Figure 2. Learning Web on Grizzly Bears.

visual diagram that helps show the relationships among key concepts. (See Figure 2.)

The students gather in small groups to read a series of articles about large animals. Working together, they decide which points are important enough to underline or annotate. Each group then organizes the information it has found, using the type of visual model demonstrated by the teacher the day before. Each group displays its diagram to the class as an overhead transparency, explaining the process they used to produce the diagram.

The next day, the students write summaries of the articles they have read and work together to prepare for an oral presentation to their class, using their notes and diagrams to help them plan.

- How are boundaries between subjects blurred in an activity like this one? How is this advantageous for students and for teachers?
- What function(s) does writing serve in this example?

Middle School Vignette 3

Middle school students who are originally from a dozen different countries are studying folktales using resources in English and, when available, in their primary languages. Many sources come from their classroom, school, and public libraries, but some, especially those written in the students' primary languages, come from their own homes. The students keep reflective reading journals and share responses to folktales they have read in small groups. As a class, the students read selected folktales together and watch videotaped dramatizations of several stories made by previous classes. Watching these tapes excites the students as they see stories from many different cultures being brought to life by their peers. Their teacher models different storytelling techniques, including puppetry, readers' theater, and role-playing.

After a week of reading a number of different stories, the students each select one special story to present to the class. Each student chooses the mode of storytelling that is best suited to his or her story, including staging a story as a mini-drama, drawing a picture, or creating puppets to represent key characters. Students then practice in small groups, and finally they present their folktales to the class. The teacher videotapes each presentation so that students can watch and critique their own presentations later. The videotape will also provide a model for students in next year's class.

As a further exploration of narrative, students ask their parents or caregivers to tell them stories from their own cultures. Working together, students and their parents write out these stories. In many cases, students write the stories both in their first language and in English. Figure 3 shows an example of a text written in Korean and in English. Some students also add illustrations to help classmates who speak different languages to understand and visualize their stories. The students work in groups to assemble all of these stories and create a book using the class computer. This book is duplicated so that each student has a copy. A copy is also donated to the school library so that other students may enjoy the stories and see different styles of writing from around the world.

Darling Sun and Darling Moon

A long time ago there was a widow who lived with her son and daughter. One day the mother was asked to work at a party in another village. Before the mother left she told her children, "Don't open the door for anyone."

The mother worked hard, and at the end of the day she was given rice cakes for her payment. She then started happily home. Halfway home the mother met a tiger. The tiger said, "The rice cakes smell good." The mother fearfully gave the rice cakes to the tiger and ran for home. The tiger ate the rice cakes and then ran after the mother. He soon caught up with her and killed her. Next the tiger put on the mother's dress and continued to her house.

The children were waiting for their mother. When they saw the tiger coming wearing their mother's dress, they quickly climbed a tree. The tiger saw them and started climbing after them. The children prayed to God to help them. Suddenly a rope appeared. The children hurriedly climbed the rope to heaven.

The tiger also prayed to God for a rope. A rope came down from heaven. The tiger started climbing the rope. However, when he was part way up, it broke. The tiger fell to its death. When the children reached heaven, the son became a moon, and the daughter became a sun.

해와달이 된 오누이

아주 먼 옛날 홀어머니가 아들 한명과 딸한명을 데리고 살고 있었다. 어느날 어머니가 다른 마을 잔치집에 가게 되었다. 어머니는 아이들을 불러놓고 이렇게 말하였다. "너희들은 내가 간 다음 문을 꼭 잠그고 내가 올때까지 아무에게도 열어주지말아라." 이렇게 말하고 어머니는 잔치집으로 갔다. 어머니는 잔치집에서 일을 잘하여 먹을 한 바구니 가득 받았다. 어머니가 좋아하면서 집으로 오는 도중에 호랑이를 만났다. "그 바구니에서 좋은 냄새가 나는군. 그것을 나에게 줘." 호랑이가 말하였다. 어머니는 할수 없이 그 바구니를 호랑이에게 주고 집을 향하여 뛰었다. 호랑이는 떡을 금방 먹어치운 후 어머니를 따라가서 어머니 마저 잡아 먹고 말았다. 또 호랑이는 어머니의 옷을 입고 아이들 마저 잡아 먹으려고 아이들이 사는 집으로 향하였다. 호랑이가 아이들 방으로 갔으나 아이들은 호랑이 인 것을 알고 도망쳐서 나무 위로 올라가 숨었다. 호랑이는 아이들을 찾아 다니다 가 나무 위에 있는 아이들을 발견하고 도끼로 나무를 찍으면서 올라 갔다. 아이들은 하늘을 향하여 기도하니 하늘에서 줄이 내려와서 아이들은 그것을 타고 하늘로 올라갔다. 호랑이도 아이들 처럼 기도하니 줄이 내려왔다. 호랑이도 그것을 타고 올라가다 줄이 끊어져서 죽었다. 하늘에 올라간 아이들은 남자아이는 달이 되고 여자아이는 해가 되었다.

Figure 3. Example of Text in English and Korean.

- In what way does this activity affirm both the students' primary languages and cultures and their work toward proficiency in English?
- How might the students use videotaping to critique their own work? How can this technique be used to incorporate assessment into the learning process?

Middle School Vignette 4

A class of eighth-grade students learns about characterization in fiction through reading Toni Cade Bambara's "Raymond's Run," a short story in which a young female protagonist comes to understand that competition and compassion cannot always coexist peacefully. The students begin by predicting the possible content of the story, based on the title, and they record these predictions (and the reasons for them) in their journals. The students listen to their teacher read the story aloud; then they read through selected passages themselves in small groups, stopping often to discuss their ideas or write in their journals.

After everyone has read the story, the teacher directs the students to write brief impressions of the story's protagonist, Squeaky, in their journals. The classmates exchange entries and discuss what they have written, sharing their first impressions of the character. The class works as a whole to generate and discuss responses to questions their teacher has written, referring often to the text of the story to support various responses.

Following this discussion, the teacher asks students to draw Squeaky as they visualize her, based on key passages they have chosen from the story. Then they make notes around their drawings, completing sentence starters provided by their teacher: "Squeaky likes . . . , Squeaky dislikes . . . , Squeaky sees the world . . . , Squeaky learns . . . ." They write the completed sentences around their drawings like captions and display their work for the class. After viewing one another's work and talking about what they have written, students write a more formal paper analyzing their responses to Squeaky's development as a character.

- What could be done in this example to expand students' literary experiences, based on their interest in the story? How might the theme of competition/winning be extended to other works or other kinds of projects?
- In this vignette the teacher selected the story and guided the students toward specific questions through cues and prompts. How might this be balanced with student-selected readings and student-guided activities?
- How does the focused approach to instruction—in which the teacher directs students' attention to a specific topic, such as character development—fit with instructional approaches that focus on students' own responses to and questions about what they are reading?

Middle School Vignette 5

On a gloomy January day, a group of students noisily enters the classroom for their writing workshop. Their teacher, who notices that this is not the first time the students have been disruptive and loud lately, comments, "I've noticed a breakdown in manners lately. What are manners, anyway? I know what adults mean by the term, but what does it mean to you?" Her questions stir up a conversation she could not have expected.

After a few awkward moments, one boy offers a definition: "Treating people kindly." The ice is broken, and students' responses begin to flow. Within a few minutes, the focus of the students' conversation turns to unruly behavior on the school bus and how a lack of manners there is affecting everyone. "It's sometimes so bad," says one new girl in the class, "that I worry about my little sister who's in kindergarten. What must she think of the kids fighting and cussing?" Other students confess their compliance, even participation, in the bad behavior. One quiet boy, generally a good writer and student, suggests, "It's kind of a way to keep kids off your back, if you pick on others, too. A couple times I tried to help little kids, though."

The teacher and her aide sit on the sidelines of this conversation. The talk is serious and thoughtful, and the students are listening to one another and sharing their feelings intently. They articulate very clearly their ambivalent feelings—fear of being the brunt of verbal abuse on the bus and shameful embarrassment at their own complicity. As the talk begins to wind down, the teacher asks, "How can you change this situation?"

The students agree that writing letters—to the superintendent and school board, to the principals of the schools on the bus route, and to parents' groups—would be an effective way to make their concerns known. The next day, their teacher offers a mini-lesson on appropriate format and language conventions for business letters, and suggests that the best way to get results with a letter of complaint is to offer a possible solution to the problem. The students draft and revise letters outlining several alternative solutions: hire extra adults to ride the buses; ask for parents to volunteer on a rotating basis; enlist high school seniors who are required to complete a number of hours of social work before graduation; ask the parent-teacher organization to send fliers home listing bus rules for students. The students work together for a week to revise and polish their letters, referring often to a poster on the classroom door which shows proper letter format. They work energetically and are motivated to write clearly and effectively by their personal involvement with the subject.

Within a couple of weeks, all of the students' letters have received replies, and the principal has agreed to meet with the students to discuss the issue further. The students feel that their concerns have been heard, and they hope to be able to work with the principal and superintendent to create a viable solution to their problem.

- What is a teacher's role in creating a classroom environment where students feel comfortable discussing issues like behavior on the school bus?

- How can students develop knowledge of the power of writing to serve their needs, both during the writing process and afterward?

Middle School Vignette 6

Students from eighteen different countries work together in one middle school classroom. Their teacher asks them to develop oral histories centered on experiences many of them share, such as immigrating to a new country. The class begins this project by talking about the types of questions they might want to ask family members or others they plan to interview. They agree that it is important to have a shared set of interview questions so that their oral histories fit well together in the collection they want to assemble later. A guest speaker comes to class the next day, and students practice interviewing him. They ask questions, tape-record their conversation, and learn about conducting interviews, using tape recorders, and taking notes while talking.

The students begin their own independent interviews, adapting the list of questions developed in class to their particular situations, subjects, and interviewees. Once they have completed their interviews, they shape their notes into narratives that will form part of the class oral history portfolio. They share their stories with their classmates, who offer suggestions on how to revise and add detail and focus.

One student, Monica, interviews her uncle in Spanish, then translates the transcript into English and forms it into a narrative account. Reading over her interview transcript and notes, she thinks carefully about how to translate her uncle's spoken words into writing in order to convey his meaning clearly to her classmates. After drafting her first-person narrative based on the interview, she asks her classmates to read it. They ask her questions about parts that are unclear to them and point out mechanical problems with punctuation and spelling. Monica works again to revise her story with the help of her peers' feedback. Here is a later draft of her narrative:

Problems in El Salvador

Before I left my country I was working for a long time and I couldn't finish my studies. It was very hard to live, especially when one is poor in El Salvador.

When I was a child, the war didn't exist yet until 1978–79. When the first groups formed in 1970, it wasn't so terrible, like what is happening today. You cannot go outside at night. Well, it depends on where you live. If you live in a place where the streets are dark, then you might get assassinated or kidnapped. So later in 1978, this group began to fight against the government and so on. You'll see that they didn't stop yet. They have approximately 12 years of fighting.

When I was young, the people were talking about America. Then I was dreaming of coming to the US, but I never imagined that I would be able to be here.

As the years are passing, the guerrillas and the army are fighting each other and killing innocent people. They go into houses taking the people away from their houses at night. So in the morning, they are killed already. Nobody knows who it is—the guerrillas or the army. How I wish that this war would end! I think there should be no war in the world. I feel so sad about it and I wouldn't want this to happen anywhere in the world.

Before coming to the US, I was working in the Ministry of Agriculture of Granaries. I was giving advice to the people so they can work in the land and become the owners of the land. I worked there for around 2 years. Then I decided to come to the US because I could have better opportunities of job and study.

I like El Salvador as my country but I do like the US because it is very pretty. Both of the countries are pretty. I like them a lot and wish to go just to visit my country.

- ■ What is the teacher's role in helping students recognize their primary languages as resources in their learning process?
- ■ How can teachers help students with a project like this when they do not speak a student's first language?

HIGH SCHOOL VIGNETTES

High School Vignette 1

To pull together what they have been learning about audience and voice in writing, as well as to develop their research skills, one eleventh-grade American literature class has been given an assignment to fill the trunk belonging to an imaginary great-aunt, Rachel, recently deceased, with letters. The assignment is prompted by an obituary which the students read and discuss, seeking ideas about Aunt Rachel as well as information about historical contexts. Students brainstorm the kinds of letters their imaginary aunt might have received over the course of her lifetime, from childhood and school friends, parents, boyfriends, employers, and so on. They find and study examples of published collections of letters from the period for models and clues. The students assemble a list of events, inventions, personalities, manners and social customs, fashions, and fads that might have influenced Aunt Rachel and her correspondents. They soon realize how much is involved in reconstructing everyday life in the past, and they delve further into research and reading on the Jazz Age, World War II, and the Kennedy years.

The students split into working groups of five or six, and each group chooses a decade of Aunt Rachel's life to focus on. These groups not only use library materials (newspapers from the period, historical narratives, biographies); they also interview family members and others in the community, including residents of a nearby nursing home, asking what they remember from their lives during those times. As they compile their historical materials, the students create a profile of Aunt Rachel—what she was like as a young girl, as a teacher, how she responded to social changes in the sixties, and so on. Each group prepares a presentation for the whole class, and these include a family dinner with dramatized flashbacks, a reconstructed television newscast, and a reenactment of a trip to a 1950s drive-in, complete with a cardboard Chevy and movie screen.

Adopting a specific persona, the students each write letters to Aunt Rachel. These vary from a letter from a South Pacific foxhole bearing a bullethole and the blood of a GI sweetheart wounded in the battle of Tarawa, to a letter from a third-grade nephew on wide-lined tablet paper, to a note sprinkled with peace signs from Aunt Rachel's former student turned anti-war activist in the sixties.

- How would this assignment fit with the traditional notion of research?
- How effective is this project in developing interdisciplinary connections among literature, writing, history, and social studies?
- What other types of research/inquiry projects might be effective for high school students?

High School Vignette 2

Students in one high school literature class have recently finished reading Chinua Achebe's *Things Fall Apart* and Alan Paton's *Cry, the Beloved Country*. For most of the students, these two books have been their first experience with African literature (Achebe's novel is set in colonial Nigeria, Paton's in South Africa), and they have become deeply interested in the history of Africa, its colonization by European nations, and the politics of racial apartheid in South Africa. Their engagement with the powerful drama of the two novels has led them to do further background reading on the history of Africa and its relationship to European colonialism. One group of students, in particular, has begun to notice the ways in which literary texts can offer a different view of events from what is commonly presented in historical reference works.

Many of the students have also become interested in reflecting on the parallels and differences between racial relations in Africa and their own experiences in the United States. Drawing on the personal impact of racist policies on characters in the two novels, students have opened up many conversations about the experience of racial identity and difference as it has shaped their own lives. To address the many questions they have raised, several students in the class have decided to put together a multimedia presentation for their classmates. They want to show how the novels have affected them, give their peers some background on Nigerian and South African history and culture, and dramatize their powerful emotional responses to the books and the issues raised by them.

These students are fortunate to have at their disposal a variety of media and technological resources, including CD-ROM materials on Nigerian and South African geography, history, and culture, several computer workstations, a video camera, and multimedia presentation software that will allow them to prepare their presentation for the class. Together they decide what each of their roles will be in producing their presentation. One team within the group decides to focus on dance, and they videotape one of their classmates, a dancer, performing an interpretive ballet based on Nigerian music. Another team creates maps of Nigeria and South Africa, using hypertext "hot-buttons" to incorporate historical text into their visual maps. As a group, the students listen to recordings of some of the many different types of African music, selecting and editing pieces that will enhance their visual and textual materials. Two of the students work together to write the script that will tie the presentation together, and they record a soundtrack that will serve as a voice-over for the entire presentation.

After two weeks of work, the presentation is assembled and shown to the whole class. The group that has made the presentation leads discussion afterward, responding to many of their classmates' questions about African countries and their literature.

Standards for the English Language Arts

At the end of class, they distribute an annotated bibliography of literary and historical works on modern Africa.

- How might teachers modify this project for a classroom that did not have such rich technological resources? How are the students empowered to do different things by the technology?

- What can a teacher do to create a literature classroom in which students' experiences and concerns, particularly those relating to issues like racism, can be openly and honestly addressed?

- What works of American literature might be effective in conjunction with the African novels used in this class?

High School Vignette 3

Sharon, a student in a high school writing workshop, is looking over the draft of a character sketch of her grandfather. Her essay was discussed in peer revision group the day before, and she is going through the paper, looking for places to insert more sensory detail and descriptive language.

Her teacher joins Sharon in analyzing the paper. "I can see by your writing-group evaluation sheet that the group gave you lots of useful revision suggestions," the teacher observes. "I really liked the way you described your grandpa's house. I can see all those magazines and newspapers stacked up around his rocking chair. But I wonder if you could tell me a little more about how he looked, what you *see* when you think of him."

"Well, I said right here that he was bent over," Sharon says, pointing to the middle of her first page.

"Yes, but I still can't quite see him—all I see is a bent-over outline. Was he all wrinkled and old? Big or small-boned?"

"Well, you see, he's only sixty but he's all bent over because he didn't drink his milk when he was a boy. They didn't have milk for him to drink. And he worked pulling tobacco since he was four—ruined his back."

"Pulling tobacco? What's that?"

"That means picking tobacco, which is done by pulling off the yellowed leaves from the bottom of the stalk."

"Yes, I can visualize that. But how will your reader know what you just told me?"

Sharon and her teacher discuss strategies for generating and incorporating descriptive material in a paper. Sharon decides to use the "web" technique. She writes the word *grandpa* in the center of a sheet of paper and begins adding words and images that come to mind, circling each one and connecting it to *grandpa* in the center: *bent*, *tobacco*, etc. She then fills in more details under each word, using the words as prompts for further images and language, and so on, until she's filled two pages with sensory detail. Sharon then returns to her paper to search for places to insert the new material she has generated.

- What other techniques can be useful to engage students more deeply with revision? How can teachers help students discover the creativity of the revising and editing stages?

- What considerations should be taken into account when deciding what and how much direction to give a particular writing student?

- What other ways can peer groups be useful in a writing class? How can peer groups work effectively during different phases in the writing process?

High School Vignette 4

Scott, a student in an eleventh-grade literature class studying modern poetry, has been reading and discussing William Stafford's poem "Traveling through the Dark." Here is an excerpt from his reading log that focuses on the poem:

> I read this poem three times, without stopping to write. I know I should have stopped to write down my responses, but I just kept reading it again and again. It's about a man who finds a dead deer on the side of the road at night. Here's my response after my third reading.
>
> stanza 1: He says "it is usually best to roll them into the canyon." I thought you were supposed to leave them there and report it to the police or forest rangers. Why does he make it his business to roll the deer off the side of the road? I wouldn't want to touch a dead animal. But I guess he's used to it and cares about animals. Maybe I could get used to it.
>
> stanza 3: He is surprised that the cold deer has a warm belly and then he realizes that there is a baby deer alive inside waiting to be born. The dead deer is pregnant! How awful and sad ". . . never to be born." I was shocked when I read this part the first time.
>
> stanza 4: He says he turned red. Why? He says "around our group, I could hear the wilderness listen." What group? He and the dead deer and the baby inside its dead mother? Yes, because he is alone. The poem says at the beginning that "I found a deer"—not "we."
>
> stanza 5: He pushes the deer over the cliff or bank into the river. Why? Couldn't he get somebody to operate and save the baby? What does he mean when he says "I thought hard for all of us"?
>
> This is a sad poem and not hard to understand, except I don't agree with the way the man acted. Couldn't he try to save the unborn deer? How could he just dump the mother deer with her baby into the river? Yet he seems to think he's doing the right thing. Who is the speaker of the poem? Is it the poet?
>
> I just reread the poem again. He says in the end that he "thought hard for all of us." What he means by that is that he thought what the mother and baby and he all would want. And I guess he figures that the baby couldn't live without its mother and would be better off dying with her. So he let it die inside where it feels at home.

Scott's teacher has the class go further in responding to the poem. The students discuss their readings and responses in small groups, then as a whole class. Finally they use what they've learned by reading and responding alone and with others to craft an essay showing how their responses to the poem tell them something about themselves. Scott's finished essay reads as follows:

Response to William Stafford's
"Traveling through the Dark"

This is a poem about a man who is driving along a country road at night and sees

a dead deer by the side of the road. He gets out of his car to push the deer into the canyon off the narrow road. He is concerned that other drivers might swerve to avoid the dead deer and then have accidents, possibly killing themselves or their passengers or people in oncoming cars. When he starts to move the deer he feels that its belly is warm. Then he realizes that the dead deer is a mother with an unborn fawn alive inside her. The man thinks for a while and then pushes the deer off the bank into the river.

When I first read this poem I thought the man was cruel to dump the dead deer in the river with its unborn baby inside. I wondered why he didn't operate on the mother or call a vet. But after many readings I realized that the man did what he thought the mother and baby would want him to do. It was hard for him to make the right decision. He says he "thought hard for all of us." He means for the two deer and for himself and maybe for the rest of us too. In the next to the last stanza the man says he stood by his car "turning red." Does that refer to the light of the tail-light of his car? Maybe it also tells us how bad he felt about the situation. So in the end he did what he felt was right about the two deer, because he cared so much about them. I wonder if he is also trying to say that what he did was "for us" too, but how could it have been for us?

I don't know if I could do what the man in the poem did and I'm not sure he did the right thing. But he was trying to do what he thought best and most kind.

- How can teachers ensure that their classrooms are safe environments in which many different perspectives on an ethical issue can be expressed?

- How might literature groups be structured and monitored for this assignment and others like it?

- What poems might be paired with Stafford's to serve as touchstones for other students or to represent other moral dilemmas?

High School Vignette 5

Students in a high school literature class are watching a scene from Tony Richardson's film version of *Hamlet*. This is the third clip of the "Get thee to a nunnery" scene they have watched since they finished reading the play; the other two were directed by Rodney Bennett and Laurence Olivier. Their teacher is using film versions of the play to help the students experience *Hamlet* on a more personal level. He challenges them to use what they see in the clips to answer the question, "What does Hamlet know of the plotting of Claudius and Polonius, and when does he know it?"

In Richardson's scene, Hamlet encounters Ophelia lounging in a hammock, and they exchange playful endearments. The camera work is tight, consisting of two-shots and close-ups. Hamlet coyly moves beneath Ophelia's hammock to woo her from the other side, and the camera captures the chemistry between the two. At first, Hamlet's words "Get thee to a nunnery" seem almost protective, as if a cloistered sanctuary might save Ophelia from what Hamlet believes will be an uncertain and disturbing future. But the camera pulls back to reveal Polonius spying on the pair from behind a partition. Hamlet, noticing a sudden movement, suspects that he has been set up by Ophelia and responds with bitter fury, shouting, "Where's your father?" Ophelia's response is ambiguous. Hamlet's anger shocks her, and when he departs with the line "To a nunnery, go," Ophelia poignantly responds, "O, what a noble mind is here o'erthrown!"

The students are unsure, based on Ophelia's expression in this scene, whether she was aware of her father's presence. One student expresses her belief that Ophelia would not have reacted with tears had she been aware all along that she and Hamlet were being watched. But another points out that in the text of the play, Ophelia is present when the king instructs Polonius to eavesdrop on the pair. "What gives the director the right to change the play like that?" she asks. This comment prompts a return to the text for evidence, encouraging close reading and lively discussion.

Another issue raised by the film is the possibility of multiple "correct" interpretations of a work. Is Olivier's shortened version any less *Hamlet* than Richardson's?

These questions concerning interpretation become central to the students when they are given the opportunity to play director themselves. One group of students is assigned the third scene—the "closet" scene—which the class will examine the next day. They are to describe the scene from the perspective of a director, choosing particular actors, advising them on emphasis and tone, and blocking the physical interactions between Hamlet and his mother. This project helps the students to visualize the scene and to interpret the images and lines for themselves and their classmates.

As a further extension of the project, the students develop storyboards for particular scenes from the play. This requires them to think through the scene differently, from a camera's point of view, dividing the action into frames and deciding who and what will be the focus. They must think about camera angle, lighting, framing, set design, and all the elements of both film and drama. The students complete their discussion of *Hamlet* by presenting their completed storyboards to their classmates and discussing choices they have made in designing their own scenes.

- In what other ways might film be used to help students explore and interpret difficult literary texts?
- What would be lost or gained by substituting a traditional essay for the storyboard project as a mode of student response to *Hamlet?*
- What other activities and projects might teachers use to teach Shakespeare to high school students?

■　■　■

These vignettes illustrate a variety of classroom practices and projects, in which students' perspectives, interests, and needs shape classroom discussion, writing projects, and curriculum choices. These illustrations clearly show the interconnections among the six English language arts. While many of the examples focus primarily on reading, writing, or speaking, for example, these are not isolated from other components of visual and spoken language use.

The vignettes also offer positive examples of interdisciplinary learning. In many of the classrooms portrayed above, the English language arts serve as a gateway into other subjects such as history, social studies, art history, geography, even zoology. We encourage readers to work with colleagues in other disciplines to develop connections among traditionally distinct content areas and to help students' literacy grow in relation to their work in an array of subjects.

In choosing the classroom examples for this chapter, we have sought to provide views of different types of classrooms and different types of students. We recognize that some schools are richly endowed with reference materials and technological resources, while others have limited resources. So, too, we realize that many schools are demographically and linguistically diverse, while others are more homogeneous in their makeup. We therefore offer these vignettes as starting points for discussion, and we encourage teachers, parents, administrators, and other readers to consider them in light of the particular needs of their students and communities.

Another theme that carries through all of these classroom portraits is the teacher's role in closely observing students. Judgments about how and how well students are learning, and about the extent to which they are achieving the standards, need to be made by those who see them working with language every day. In response to questions about how progress toward the standards is to be evaluated, we strongly reaffirm the role of the teacher. By watching students closely, reflecting on their development, and guiding them when they need help, teachers both assess and advance their students' progress.

IN CONCLUSION

This document describes what we—the International Reading Association and the National Council of Teachers of English—believe students should know about and be able to do with language by the time they reach the end of their secondary schooling. The twelve content standards we have proposed grow out of a national conversation about the goals and purposes of English language arts education. Our aim is to ensure that all students develop the literacy skills they need to succeed in school and in various areas of life.

Many observers worry about the act of defining standards for the English language arts and other subject areas, fearing that the result will be to restrict the creativity and flexibility that characterize good teaching and learning. This concern goes to the heart of the tradition of public schooling in the United States.

Throughout our nation's history there have been periodic attempts to define a national agenda for the schools, yet decisions about what should be taught and how it should be taught have always been made by local teachers and administrators in response to local needs and concerns. This is the way it should be, we believe, and these standards should not be seen as a veiled (or unveiled) attempt to undermine that tradition.

Rather, we urge a more positive view of standard-setting. We feel strongly that guidelines for English language arts education are necessary because they provide a clear map of the goals of schooling. This clarity of purpose is particularly important in our current political and economic climate, in which public expectations of the schools, as well as criticisms of their work, are increasing. Standards offer a way to guide and support the best practices in English language arts education. In addition to this document, IRA and NCTE have prepared several documents showing classroom practices using these standards.

As we discussed at the outset, we also believe that standards are needed to prepare students for the literacy requirements of the future as well as the present. If we are to prepare all students to become proficient users of language, and if we are to bridge the great disparities that exist in educational opportunities, then standards are a necessary part of that effort.

This final point is particularly important. We do not imagine that setting standards is, by itself, sufficient to address the problems that beset our

Decisions about what should be taught and how it should be taught have always been made in response to local needs and concerns, and these standards should not be seen as a veiled (or unveiled) attempt to undermine that tradition.

Standards for the English Language Arts

nation's schools. Perhaps one of the greatest challenges to the attainment of these standards is the plague of unequal opportunities and expectations. Some students in our country have abundant resources for learning: they attend schools that are well equipped with books as well as technological and human resources; they have every opportunity to achieve high levels of competency in all areas of the curriculum. Others, however, are far less fortunate. Neither the most forceful and eloquent standards in the world, nor the most dedicated teachers, can overcome these barriers.

These standards represent not an end but a beginning—a starting point for discussion and action within states, districts, and individual schools across the country. Quality education can only happen, we believe, when it is fostered by local conversations. Teachers and school administrators must translate these standards for themselves, considering and responding to the particular needs of their students and communities. To make certain that our national conversation continues, we are asking you to complete and return the survey form in Appendix F. If this book encourages fertile debate about the means and ends of English language arts education, then its central aims will have been achieved.

Wise understanding tends to consist of the ability to see and affirm the truth of contrary points of view.
—Peter Elbow,
Embracing Contraries

GLOSSARY

The following terms are used in the preceding chapters or are closely related to concepts presented there.

aesthetic   Pertaining to judgments of beauty or formal appropriateness, originality, or interest. Traditionally, the "aesthetic dimensions" of literary response have been associated with the reflective contemplation of the literary text as an artistic work in itself, apart from social and historical contexts. However, the standards presented here are founded on the assumption that an aesthetic experience results from a reading event that mutually involves and is influenced by the reader and the text in a particular context. The reader brings to the text internalized language and life experiences, which in the encounter with the text create a new experience. Thus interpretation of a literary work depends not only on the text itself, but also on the reader's ideas and feelings evoked during engagement with the text.

analysis   The process or result of identifying the parts of a whole and their relationships to one another.

appreciation   Thoughtful awareness of value; personal understanding and respect for; judgments made with heightened perception and understanding. Literary appreciation goes beyond simple comprehension to involve personal or moral judgment, artistic awareness, and emotional investment in a work or performance.

assessment standards   **1.** Statements setting forth guidelines for evaluating student work, as in the *Standards for the Assessment of Reading and Writing* (see Appendix E). **2.** Measures of student performance.

audience   The collection of intended readers, listeners, or viewers for a particular work or performance. An audience may be physically present (in the case of a dramatic performance or speech) or separated by time and distance (in the case of written texts).

authentic   Something that is meaningful because it reflects or engages the real world. An *authentic task* asks students to do something they might really have to do in the course of their lives, or to apply certain knowledge or skills to situations they might really encounter.

canon   The body of literary or other artistic works that a given culture defines as important at a given time; that is, works perceived by that culture to express significant values and to exemplify artistic excellence.

CD-ROM   Compact disc with read-only memory. A computer add-on used in place of a floppy disk and disk drive because it has a much larger storage capacity for text, graphics, sound, and computer programs.

classic texts   Literary or other works (e.g., films, speeches) that have been **canonized**, either continuously or intermittently, over a period of time beyond that of their initial publication and reception.

cognitive process   Process by which readers, writers, and viewers actively construct meaning as they engage with texts by organizing, selecting, and connecting information; making inferences; and performing acts of **interpretation**.

communication   The meaningful exchange of ideas or information between a speaker and a listener (or a reader and a writer, etc.). Communication may be primarily functional ("Pass me the salt"), primarily **expressive** ("To be, or not to be"), or some combination of the two. Throughout these standards, communication is understood as an interactive process, in which both speaker and listener participate in the **construction of meaning**.

comprehension   The construction of the meaning of a written, spoken, or visual communication through a reciprocal interchange of ideas between the receiver and the composer; comprehension occurs within and is influenced by the immediate **context**.

constructing meaning   The process by which readers (meant here in the term's broadest sense) create meaning for the texts they read, view, or listen to. These meanings are built from the connections the reader makes between the new material and his or her **prior knowledge**, the ways the reader structures meaning, and decisions the reader makes about what is important or relevant.

contemporary texts   Literary or other works that have been written in recent years; they frequently address issues and events of current concern to a given community but may also be broader in scope or retrospective in content.

content   One of three dimensions in our conceptual model for the English language arts standards, content refers to *what* students should learn in the English language arts. The content dimension addresses what students should know and be able to do with respect to the English language arts. This includes knowledge of spoken, visual, and written **texts** and of the processes involved in creating, critiquing, and interpreting such texts.

content standards   Statements of what students should know and be able to do in a given discipline, here the English language arts.

context   **1.** The sounds, words, or phrases adjacent to a spoken or written language unit; linguistic environment. **2.** The social or cultural situation in which a spoken or written message occurs.

convention   **1.** An accepted practice in a spoken or written language. **2.** An accepted way of creating an effect, as the soliloquy in drama, the flashback in fiction.

critical reading   Reading a text in such a way as to question assumptions, explore perspectives, and critique underlying social and political values or stances. Critical reading is resistant, active, and focused on both the text and the world. Critical readers bring a range of experiences to texts, and, in turn, use texts to develop critical perspectives on personal and social experience.

critical thinking   The thought processes characteristic of creativity, criticism, and logic in literature, the arts, science, and other disciplines; divergent thinking.

cues   Various sources of information used by readers to construct meaning. The language cueing systems include the graphophonic (also referred to as graphophonemic) system—the relationships between oral and written language (**phonics**); the syntactic system—the relationship among linguistic units such as prefixes, suffixes, words, phrases, and clauses (**grammar**); and the **semantic** system—the meaning system of language. Reading strategies and language cueing systems are also influenced by pragmatics—the knowledge readers have about the ways in which language is understood by others in their culture.

curriculum   **1.** The actual opportunities for learning provided at a particular place and time. **2.** The total program of formal studies offered by a school. **3.** All the educational experiences planned for and provided by a school. **4.** A particular part of the program of studies of a school, as the English curriculum, the reading curriculum.

decode **1.** To analyze spoken or graphic symbols of a familiar language to ascertain their intended meaning. **2.** To change communication signals into messages, as to decode body language.

development One dimension of our conceptual model, *development* refers to *how* students grow as language users. The development dimension focuses on the ways in which learners develop competencies in the language arts.

dialect A social or regional variety of a particular language with phonological, grammatical, and lexical patterns that distinguish it from other varieties.

diversity The multitude of differing viewpoints and perspectives—based at least in part on gender, race, culture, **ethnicity**, or religion—in the United States and the world.

emergent literacy Development of the association of print with meaning that begins early in a child's life and continues until the child reaches the stage of conventional reading and writing.

ethnicity Affiliation with any of the large groups of people commonly classified by language, race, national or geographic origin, culture, or religion.

evaluation **1.** The use of **critical reading** and **critical thinking** to judge and assign meaning or importance to a particular experience or event. **2.** The process used by teachers and students to appraise and judge achievement, growth, product, and process or changes in these, frequently through the use of formal and informal tests and techniques.

expressive text Written, spoken, or visual creation that reveals or explores the author's thoughts, feelings, and observations—for example, in questions, comments, journal entries, logs, or freewriting.

fiction Imaginative literary, oral, or visual works representing invented, rather than actual, persons, places, and events. Widely recognized **genres** of fiction include mystery, romance, and adventure.

figurative language Any language, whether in a literary or a nonliterary text, using figures of speech such as **metaphor** or hyperbole to create multiple or intensified meanings.

fluency The clear, rapid, and easy expression of ideas in writing or speaking; movements that flow smoothly, easily, and readily.

genre A category used to classify literary and other works, usually by form, technique, or content. Categories of **fiction** such as mystery, science fiction, romance, or adventure are considered genres.

grammar The means by which the different components of language can be put together in groups of sounds and written or visual symbols so that ideas, feelings, and images can be communicated; what one knows about the structure and use of one's own language that leads to its creative and communicative use.

graphophonic/graphophonemic One of three cueing systems readers use to construct texts; the relationships between oral and written language (**phonics**).

home language The language or languages learned and used by children in their homes and communities both before and after their entry into school. The term may refer both to national languages and to varieties of English and other languages.

image *Note: Image* is a general term with many shades of meaning but usually implies a physical or mental resemblance. An image may be concrete or abstract. It may be based on experience or imagination. It may refer to sensory experiences, especially visual ones, or to any physical or ideational representation of such experiences. **1.** A mental representation of something, usually incomplete; impression. **2.** A description in speech or writing. **3.** A figure of speech, especially a simile or **metaphor**.

imagery **1.** The process or result of forming mental images while reading or listening to a story, viewing a film, etc. **2.** The use of language to create sensory impressions, as the imagery of the phrase "such sweet sorrow." **3.** Collectively, the **figurative language** in a work. **4.** The study of image patterns in **literature** for clues to the text's deeper meaning.

inquiry A mode of research driven by the learner's desire to look deeply into a question or an idea that interests him or her.

integrated language arts A **curricular** organization in which students study and use the language components of speaking, listening, reading, and writing as a mutually reinforcing process that evolves through a unified core of concepts and activities.

interpretation **1.** The process of inferring beyond the literal meaning of a communication. **2.** The analysis of the meaning of a communication. *Note:* In this context, interpretation involves both **grammatical** and **semantic** analysis and the interplay between them. **3.** A performance, usually artistic, to which the performer gives distinctive meaning.

language diversity Variety in both national languages and **dialects** or codes within national languages. Our understanding of language diversity in this document recognizes the historical, cultural, religious, and personal meanings that these different languages and forms of language carry within them.

linguistic patterns The characteristics of **syntax**, diction, **vocabulary**, or degrees of elaboration that may vary according to social and cultural **context**.

linguistics **1.** The study of the nature and structure of language and languages. **2.** The study of the nature of language communication.

listening Attending to communication by any means; includes listening to vocal speech, watching signing, or using communication aids.

literacy The standards outlined in this document reflect a contemporary view of literacy that is both broader and more demanding than traditional definitions. Until quite recently, literacy was generally defined, in a very limited way, as the ability to read or write one's own name. A much more ambitious definition of literacy today includes the capacity to accomplish a wide range of reading, writing, speaking, and other language tasks associated with everyday life.

literacy community A group of language users, whether within the classroom or outside, who share a common language and a common set of concerns. Students in the classroom work together as a literacy community to read, listen to, and view their classmates' and others' works, to articulate and negotiate meanings, and to foster one another's **development**.

literary analysis The careful, detailed reading and study of a literary work by a critic, student, or scholar.

literature Imaginative writings in prose or verse, as poems, plays, novels, and short stories. Although in its modern usage *literature* is distinguished from historical writing, and increasingly from such popular forms as romance or mystery **fiction**, in this document we use a broad definition of literature that includes often excluded forms such as essays, journals, and autobiographies.

media The various physical means through which information may be communicated or **aesthetic** forms created, for example, newspapers, film, books, computer software, painting.

metaphor   A figure of speech in which the denotative word or phrase (e.g., *train*) is replaced by another word or phrase which, though not literally true, suggests a likeness or analogy (e.g., *iron horse*). In addition to being a significant element of literary expression, metaphor is also a constituent of many other kinds of language.

miscues   Unexpected responses cued by readers' knowledge of their language and concepts of the world. Miscues are not random errors, but result from attempts by readers to construct meaning as they engage with **texts**.

moral   Referring to the rules of behavior, or of right and wrong, that are accepted within a certain social group, rules that may be based on religious, ethical, or philosophical systems of belief.

multimedia   Incorporating or making use of more than one **medium**. For example, a multimedia research project might include a written report, photographs, computer-generated charts, and audiotaped interviews.

narrative   Text in any form (print, oral, or visual) that recounts events or tells a story.

National Academy of Education   Association founded at Stanford University in 1965 as a forum for educational research and discussion. Publisher of *The Nation's Report Card: Improving the Assessment of Student Achievement*.

nonprint text   Any text that creates meaning through sound or images or both, such as photographs, drawings, collages, films, videos, computer graphics, speeches, oral poems and tales, and songs.

opportunity-to-learn standards   Statements of the basic conditions necessary for students to be able to achieve **content** or **performance standards**. These may include statements concerning learning environment, equity, and access to resources.

outcome   Knowledge, skills, and understandings students gain as a result of education and experience.

performance-based assessment   The measurement of educational achievement by tasks that are similar or identical to those that are required in the instructional environment, as in performance assessment tasks, exhibitions, or projects, or in work that is assembled over time into portfolio collections.

performance standards   Statements that attempt to specify the quality of student performance at various levels of competency in the subject matter set out in the **content standards**.

phonics   Generally used to refer to the system of sound-letter relationships used in reading and writing. Phonics begins with the understanding that each letter (or grapheme) of the English alphabet stands for one or more sounds (or phonemes).

print awareness   In emergent literacy, a learner's growing awareness of print as a system of meaning, distinct from speech and visual modes of representation.

print text   Any text that creates meaning through writing, such as books, stories, reports, essays, poems, play scripts, notes, and letters. Print texts may also be produced and circulated electronically.

prior knowledge   Knowledge that stems from previous experience. *Note:* Prior knowledge is a key component of schema theories of reading comprehension in spite of the redundancy inherent in the term.

punctuation   An orthographic system that separates linguistic units, clarifies meaning, and can be used by writers and readers to give speech characteristics to written material.

purpose   One dimension of our conceptual model for the English language arts standards, *purpose* refers to *why* students use the language arts. In particular, we recommend a focus in English language arts education on four purposes of language use: for obtaining and communicating information, for literary response and expression, for learning and reflection, and for problem solving and application.

reading   The complex, **recursive** process through which we make meaning from texts, using **semantics**; **syntax**; visual, aural, and tactile cues; **context**; and **prior knowledge**. *Note:* In *Standards for the English Language Arts, reading* refers to **listening** and **viewing** in addition to print-oriented reading. Learners with visual or other impairments may read by means of, for example, braillers, sign language, magnification devices, and closed-captioned television.

recode   To change a message into symbols, as recoding oral language into writing, or recoding an idea into words.

recursive   Characterized by moving back and forth through a document in either **reading** it or creating it, as new ideas are developed or problems encountered. In reading a text, recursive processes might include rereading earlier portions in light of later ones, looking ahead to see what topics are addressed or how a narrative ends, and skimming through text to search for particular ideas or events before continuing a linear reading. In creating a written composition, recursive processes include moving back and forth among the planning, drafting, and revising phases of writing.

reflection   **1.** The process or result of seriously thinking over one's experiences. **2.** An approach to problem solving that emphasizes the careful consideration of the nature of the problem, the thorough planning of procedures to solve the problem, and the monitoring of the processes used in reaching a solution.

rhetoric   **1.** The art or science of using language in prose or verse. **2.** The effective use of language in oratory to influence or persuade an **audience**. **3.** The study of the theory and principles of effective **communication**.

rhetorical devices   Any of the techniques used by writers to communicate meaning or to persuade an **audience**. Rhetorical devices range from word- or sentence-level techniques such as the use of **metaphor** or apostrophe (direct address to the reader) to techniques that shape an entire piece, such as irony or extended analogy.

semantics   One of three cueing systems readers use to construct texts. The semantic system focuses on the meaning of texts, where meaning is seen as connections between words (or other linguistic units) and the reader's **prior knowledge** of language and linguistic forms, understanding of the world, and experience of other **texts** and **contexts**.

speaking   The act of communicating through such means as vocalization, signing, or using communication aids such as voice synthesizers.

spelling   The process of representing language by means of a writing system, or orthography.

standard English   **1.** That variety of English in which most educational texts and government and media publications are written in the United States. *Note:* Also referred to as *the language of wider communication* in this document. **2.** English as it is spoken and written by those groups with social, economic, and political power in the United States. *Note:* Standard English is a relative concept, varying widely in pronunciation and idiomatic use but maintaining a fairly uniform grammatical structure.

standards   Statements about what is valued in a given field, such as English language arts, and/or descriptions of what is considered quality work. See **content standards**, **assessment standards**, and **performance standards**.

strategy   A practiced but flexible way of responding to recognizable **contexts**, situations, or demands. Because no single reading strategy, study technique, or **writ-**

ing process is best for all students, it is inappropriate to teach a single way of approaching all language tasks. Instead, we must help every student to acquire a range of strategies and to learn how to choose and apply those that best fit his or her needs and the literacy situation at hand.

style **1.** The characteristics of a work that reflect its author's distinctive way of writing. **2.** An author's use of language, its effects, and its appropriateness to the author's intent and theme. **3.** The manner in which something is said or done, in contrast to its message, as Hemingway's terse, blunt, conversational style. **4.** The particular way in which a person uses language in a given social environment.

syntax **1.** One of three cueing systems readers use to construct texts; the syntactic system focuses on the relationship among linguistic units such as prefixes, suffixes, words, phrases, and clauses (**grammar**). **2.** The study of how sentences are formed and of the grammatical rules that govern their formation. **3.** The pattern or structure of word order in sentences, clauses, and phrases.

synthesis The process of identifying the relationships among two or more ideas or other textual elements.

technological communication Communication by means of the newer technologies of film, videotape, and electronic media (such as e-mail and the World Wide Web).

technological resource An informational resource using newer technologies such as computer software, computer networks, databases, **CD-ROMs**, and laser discs.

text In the *Standards for the English Language Arts* we use the term *text* broadly to refer to printed communications in their varied forms; oral communications, including conversations, speeches, etc.; and visual communications such as film, video, and computer displays.

text structure The temporal and spatial arrangement of elements in a written, oral, or visual text. For example, the text structure of a **narrative** film might involve moving back and forth among different time periods in recounting events; or the text structure of an argumentative essay might involve a linear arrangement of definitions, arguments, evidence, counterarguments, and rebuttal.

textual features Characteristics of print texts such as sound-letter correspondence, sentence structure, and **context**.

tone The implied attitude toward the subject matter or **audience** of a text that readers may infer from the text's language, **imagery**, and structure.

usage The way in which the native language or **dialect** of a speech community is actually used by its members.

viewing Attending to communication conveyed by **visually representing**. Students with visual impairments might "view" tactile drawings, charts, or diagrams.

visually representing Conveying information or expressing oneself using nonverbal visual means, such as drawing, computer graphics (maps, charts, artwork), photography, or physical performance. For students with visual impairments, this language art might also include communicating by means of tactile drawings or diagrams, as well as by gesture and performance.

vocabulary Those words known or used by a person or group, including the specialized meanings that words acquire when they are used for technical purposes, regional usages, and slang.

word recognition **1.** The quick and easy identification of the form, pronunciation, and appropriate meaning of a word previously met in print or writing. **2.** The process of determining the pronunciation and some degree of meaning of a word in written or printed form.

writing   **1.** The use of a writing system or orthography by people in the conduct of their daily lives to communicate over time and space. **2.** The process or result of recording language graphically by hand or other means, as by the use of computers or braillers.

writing process   The many aspects of the complex act of producing a written communication; specifically, planning, drafting, revising, editing, and publishing.

REFERENCES

Australian Education Council & National Council of Ministers of Education. (1994). Key assumptions underlying the English profile. In *English—A curriculum profile for Australian schools*. Carlton, Australia: Curriculum Corporation.

DeFabio, R. Y. (1994). *Outcomes in process: Setting standards for language use*. Portsmouth, NH: Heinemann.

Delaware Department of Public Instruction. (1995). Glossary of terms. In *New directions: State of Delaware English language arts curriculum framework*. Dover, DE: Author.

Flood, J., Jensen, J., Lapp, D., & Squire, J. R. (Eds.). (1991). *Handbook of research on teaching in the English language arts*. IRA and NCTE.

Harris, T. L., & Hodges, R. E. (Eds.). (1995). *The literacy dictionary: The vocabulary of reading and writing*. Newark, DE: IRA.

Holman, H. C., & Harmon, W. (1992). *A handbook to literature* (6th ed.). New York: Macmillan.

Lentricchia, F., & McLaughlin, T. (Eds.). (1990). *Critical terms for literary study*. Chicago: University of Chicago Press.

Nevada Department of Education. (1994). Glossary. In *Nevada English language arts framework* (Draft 2). Carson City, NV: Author.

New Zealand Ministry of Education. (1994). Selected glossary. In *English in the New Zealand curriculum*. Wellington, New Zealand: Learning Media, Ltd.

Ohio Department of Education, Division of Curriculum, Instruction, and Professional Development. (1992). *Model competency-based language arts program*. Columbus, OH: Author.

Purves, A. C. (Ed.), with Papa, L., & Jordan, S. (1994). *Encyclopedia of English studies and language arts: A project of the National Council of Teachers of English*. New York: Scholastic.

Rosenblatt, L. M. (1978). *The reader, the text, the poem: The transactional theory of the literary work*. Carbondale, IL: Southern Illinois University Press.

Appendix A

LIST OF PARTICIPANTS

The following lists have been compiled as carefully as possible from available records. We apologize to anyone whom we have omitted or whose name, address, or affiliation we have misrepresented. Inclusion on these lists does not imply endorsement of this document. The following abbreviations have been used in these lists: SPELA (Standards Project for English Language Arts), IRA (International Reading Association), and NCTE (National Council of Teachers of English).

SPELA NATIONAL BOARD (October 1992–March 1994)

Janet Emig, *Chair;* Professor Emeritus, Rutgers University, New Brunswick, NJ; Tacoma, WA

Richard C. Anderson, Director, Center for the Study of Reading, University of Illinois at Urbana-Champaign

Kathryn Au, Formerly: Educational Psychologist, Kamehameha Schools, Honolulu, HI; Now: University of Hawaii, Honolulu

George Ayers, Executive Director, Council for Exceptional Children, Reston, VA

Adrienne Bailey, Superintendent of Instructional Services, Chicago Public Schools, IL

Christopher Cross, Executive Director, Educational Initiative for the Business Roundtable, Washington, DC

Lois Distad, Teacher, Bar Nunn Elementary School, Casper, WY

Pascal D. Forgione, Jr., Superintendent, Department of Public Instruction, Dover, DE

Janis Gabay, Teacher, Junipero Serra High School, San Diego, CA

Henry Louis Gates, Jr., Professor, Harvard University, Cambridge, MA

Roseann Dueñas Gonzalez, Director, Writing Skills Improvement Program, University of Arizona, Tucson

The Honorable William Goodling, Representative from Pennsylvania, United States House of Representatives, Washington, DC

Donald Hamingson, Teacher, Columbia High School, Maplewood, NJ

Shirley Brice Heath, Professor, Stanford University, Palo Alto, CA

Julie M. Jensen, Professor, University of Texas at Austin

Mary Kitagawa, Teacher, Marks Meadow Demonstration School, Amherst, MA

Arturo Madrid, Murchison Distinguished Professor of the Humanities, Trinity University, San Antonio, TX

Sharon O'Neal, Director, English Language Arts and Reading, Texas Education Agency, Austin

Katherine Paterson, Author, Barre, VT

Darzell Paz, Reading Specialist, Lake Seneca Elementary School, Germantown, MD

Jerry Pinkney, Illustrator, Croton-on-Hudson, NY

Linda Rief, Teacher, Oyster River Middle School, Durham, NH

Richard Robinson, President, Scholastic Inc., New York, NY

Robert Scholes, Professor, Brown University, Providence, RI

The Honorable Paul Simon, Senator from Illinois, United States Senate, Washington, DC

Sheila Valencia, Professor, University of Washington, Seattle

Patrick Welsh, Teacher, T. C. Williams High School, Alexandria, VA

SPELA EX OFFICIO BOARD (October 1992–March 1994)

Donna Alvermann, University of Georgia, Athens; *Co-Director, National Reading Research Center*

Arthur N. Applebee, State University of New York at Albany; *Director, National Research Center on Literature Teaching and Learning*

Miriam T. Chaplin, Rutgers University, Camden, NJ; *Past President, National Council of Teachers of English*

Beverly Ann Chin, University of Montana, Missoula; *President, National Council of Teachers of English*

Sarah W. Freedman, University of California at Berkeley; *Director, National Research Center on Writing and Literacy*

Susan Mandel Glazer, Rider College, Lawrenceville, NJ; *Past President, International Reading Association*

John Guthrie, University of Maryland, College Park; *Co-Director, National Reading Research Center*

Janie Hydrick, McArthur Elementary School, Mesa, AZ; *Past President, National Council of Teachers of English*

Barbara Kapinus, Washington, DC; *Senior Program Director, Council of Chief State School Officers*

Dolores B. Malcolm, St. Louis Public Schools, MO; *President, International Reading Association*

Barry McLaughlin, University of California-Santa Cruz; Formerly: *Co-Director, National Research Center on Cultural Diversity and Second Language Learning*

Jesse Perry, (retired), San Diego City Schools, CA; *Past President, National Council of Teachers of English*

Doris Roettger, Heartland Area Education Agency, Johnston, IA; *Past President, International Reading Association*

Roger Rogalin, New York, NY; *Associate Director, Association of American Publishers*

SPELA EARLY SCHOOL TASK FORCE (October 1992–March 1994)

Erminda García, *Chair;* Teacher, Alianza Elementary School, Watsonville, CA

Dawn Harris Martine, *Co-Chair;* Teacher, Manhattan New School, New York

Bernice Cullinan, *Executive Secretary;* Professor, New York University

Shelley Harwayne, Director, Manhattan New School, New York

Edward J. Kameenui, Professor, University of Oregon, Eugene

Irene Serna, Formerly: Professor, Arizona State University, Tempe. Now: Scottsdale Public Schools, AZ

Timothy Shanahan, Professor, University of Illinois at Chicago

Susan Stires, Teacher, Center for Teaching and Learning, Edgecomb, ME

SPELA MIDDLE SCHOOL TASK FORCE (October 1992–March 1994)

Maureen Barbieri, *Chair;* Teacher, Spartanburg Day School, Greenville, SC

Marshá Taylor DeLain, *Co-Chair;* Associate State Superintendent, Department of Public Instruction, Dover, DE

Dennie Palmer Wolf, *Executive Secretary;* Director, PACE, Harvard University, Cambridge, MA

Robert E. Probst, Professor, Georgia State University, Atlanta

Carol Santa, Coordinator, Language Arts and Social Studies, School District #5, Kalispell, MT

Carol Tateishi, Director, Bay Area Writing Project, Berkeley, CA

Edith Tony, Teacher, Chuska Boarding School, Tohatchie, NM

Richard Vacca, Professor, Kent State University, OH

SPELA HIGH SCHOOL TASK FORCE (October 1992–March 1994)

Doris Dancy, *Chair;* Teacher, Hampton High School, VA

Gwendolyn Alexander, *Co-Chair;* Instructional Specialist, Washington, DC, Public Schools

James Marshall, *Executive Secretary;* Professor, University of Iowa, Iowa City

Carmen A. Aviles, Teacher, Community High School, District 94, West Chicago, IL

Sheridan Blau, Professor, University of California at Santa Barbara

John Forsyth, Teacher, Lander Valley High School, WY

R. Stephen Green, Assistant to the Superintendent, Lawrence Township School District, Indianapolis, IN

Faith Schullstrom, Administrator, Guilderland Central School District, NY

Douglas Vance, Teacher, LaFollette High School, Madison, WI

SPELA STAFF MEMBERS (September 1992–March 1994)

Alan E. Farstrup, *Project Co-Director;* International Reading Association

Miles Myers, *Project Co-Director;* National Council of Teachers of English

P. David Pearson, *Project Co-Director;* Formerly: Center for the Study of Reading, University of Illinois at Urbana-Champaign; Now: Michigan State University, East Lansing

Jean Osborn, *Project Coordinator;* Center for the Study of Reading, University of Illinois at Urbana-Champaign

Carolyn Hill, *Project Associate;* National Council of Teachers of English

Fran Lehr, *Editor;* Center for the Study of Reading, University of Illinois at Urbana-Champaign

Anne Stallman, *Data Analyst;* University of Illinois at Urbana-Champaign

Ellen Swengel, *Conference Coordinator;* Center for the Study of Reading, University of Illinois at Urbana-Champaign

Amber Walker, *Project Staff;* University of Illinois at Urbana-Champaign

IRA PRESIDENTS (During project duration)

Judith Thelen, 1991–1992, Frostburg State University, MD

Marie Clay, 1992–1993, University of Auckland, New Zealand

Doris Roettger, 1993–1994, Heartland Area Education Agency, Johnston, IA

Susan Mandel Glazer, 1994–1995, Rider University, Lawrenceville, NJ

Dolores B. Malcolm, 1995–1996, St. Louis Public Schools, MO

Richard Vacca, 1996–1997, Kent State University, OH

John J. Pikulski, 1997–1998, University of Delaware, Newark

IRA BOARD MEMBERS (During project duration)

Joan F. Curry, 1990–1993, San Diego State University, CA

John J. Pikulski, 1990–1993, University of Delaware, Newark

Kathryn Ann Ransom, 1990–1993, Springfield Public Schools, IL

Daniel R. Hittleman, 1991–1994, Queens College, CUNY, Flushing

Donna M. Ogle, 1991–1994, National-Louis University, Evanston, IL

Pehr-Olof Rönnholm, 1991–1994, Cygnaeus School, Turku, Finland

Mabel T. Edmonds, 1992–1995, St. Louis Public Schools, MO

Linda B. Gambrell, 1992–1995, University of Maryland, College Park

Jerry L. Johns, 1992–1995, Northern Illinois University, De Kalb

Sandra McCormick, 1993–1996, Ohio State University, Columbus

MaryEllen Vogt, 1993–1996, California State University, Long Beach

Carmelita Kimber Williams, 1993–1996, Norfolk State University, VA

John Elkins, 1994–1997, University of Queensland, St. Lucia, Australia

Yetta M. Goodman, 1994–1997, University of Arizona, Tucson

Barbara J. Walker, 1994–1997, Montana State University, Billings

Richard L. Allington, 1995–1998, University at Albany-SUNY

James F. Baumann, 1995–1998, University of Georgia, Athens

Kathleen Stumpf Jongsma, 1995–1998, Northside Independent School District, San Antonio, TX

IRA STAFF (During project duration)

Alan E. Farstrup, Executive Director

Terry S. Salinger, Director of Research/Project Coordinator

Gail Keating, Projects Manager, Research

Other staff:

Janet Butler, Public Information Coordinator

Mary E. Cash, Senior Secretary, Executive Office

Matthew S. Freeman, Associate Editor, *Reading Today*

Deborah A. Moses Houston, Research Specialist

Larry Husfelt, Design Consultant

Joan M. Irwin, Director of Publications

Robert G. Jones, Director of Finance (retired December 1995)

Steven C. LaMarine, Marketing Manager

Richard Long, Washington Representative

Linda McAfee, Library and Divisional Assistant, Research

John Micklos, Jr., Editor, *Reading Today*

Boni Nash, Graphic Design Coordinator

Wendy Lapham Russ, Assistant Director of Publications

Iona Sauscermen, Production Manager

Brenda S. Townsend, Director of Professional Development

Melanie Wahl, Committee Coordinator

Tracy Webb, Marketing Manager, 1992–1995

IRA ADVISORY COMMITTEE

Morton Botel, University of Pennsylvania, Philadelphia

Jack Cassidy, Millersville State University, Millersville, PA

Jacqueline Comas, University of Maryland, Columbia

Janice A. Dole, University of Utah, Salt Lake City

Nancy Roser, University of Texas, Austin

Timothy Shanahan, University of Illinois, Chicago

IRA SPECIAL ADVISORS

Lynn B. Jenkins, Writing and Editing Consultant, Northford, CT

Michael W. Kibby, University of Buffalo–SUNY

John Kruidenier, Education Consultant, Bryn Mawr, PA

John Mayher, New York University

Jean Osborn, Center for the Study of Reading, University of Illinois at Urbana-Champaign

IRA FOCUS GROUP COORDINATORS

Elizabeth (Betty) Bowers, Rapid City, SD

Suzanne F. Clewell, Prince George County Schools, MD

Gay Fawcett, Summit County Schools, Cuyahoga Falls, OH

Gail Gayeski, Wilkes University, Wilkes-Barre, PA

Patricia Mulcahy-Ernt, College Reading & Learning Association, Bridgeport, CT

Sharon O'Neal, Texas Education Agency, Austin

Maurine V. Richardson, University of South Dakota, Vermillion

IRA STATE STANDARDS COORDINATORS

Tara Azwell, Emporia State University, KS

Nancy A. Becher, Hofstra University, West Islip, NY

Karen L. Benner, Meeker School District RE-1, CO

Cindy Bowen, Baltimore County Public Schools, MD

Benita Buckles, G. C. Burkhead School, Elizabethtown, KY

George Canney, University of Idaho, Moscow

Angela Carducci, Teacher/Textbook Consultant, Las Vegas, NV

Barbara Carruthers, North Carolina Department of Public Instruction, Raleigh

JoAnn M. Carter, University of Sciences and Arts of Oklahoma, Tuttle

Cathy Chaney, Dutch Fork Elementary School, Irmo, SC

Char Hallmann Cieply, Wheeling School District #21, IL

Don Collins, Franklin West Supervisory Union, Fairfax, VT

Genny Cramer, Southern Missouri State University, Springfield

Suzanne G. Curry, Red Clay School District, Wilmington, DE

Ruth Davison, Boothbay Regional Elementary School, ME

Cheryl H. DeVenney, Caledonia High School, Columbus, MS

Marie DiBiasio, Rhode Island State Department of Education, Providence

Gay Fawcett, Summit County Schools, Cuyahoga Falls, OH

Mary Beth Fletcher, Buckingham Browne Nichols School, Cambridge, MA

Kate Friesner, College of Santa Fe, Albuquerque, NM

Kathryn F. Groller, School District of the City of Allentown, PA

Robert L. Harrison, Jr., West Virginia State Department of Education, Charleston

Dolores Heiden, University of Wisconsin, Onalaska

Ceil Hogan, Hamden Hall County Day School, Hamden, CT

Hazel H. Jessee, Virginia Beach City Public Schools, VA

Virginia Juettner, Anchorage School District, AK

Jane A. Kearns, Manchester Public Schools, NH

Colleen Kryszak, Lowell Elementary, Tacoma, WA

Gregg Kurek, Bridgman Public Schools, St. Joseph, MI

Karen S. Kutiper, Southwest Texas State University, San Marcos

Jill Lewis, Jersey City State College, NJ

Norman C. Machart, Valley City, ND

Bonnie Martinson, Morris Bye Elementary School, Coon Rapids, MN

Betty Jo McCarty, Florida State University, Panama City

Anita McClain, Pacific University, Forest Grove, OR

Coleen McClanahan, Iowa Department of Education, Des Moines

Mary R. Mills (retired), Muscogee County School District, Columbus, GA

Kay Moore, California State University, Sacramento

Lynn Oltmanns Olson, Morton Elementary School, Omaha, NE

Lillian R. Putnam (retired), Mountain Lakes, NJ

Marguerite C. Radencich, Day County School Board, Miami, FL

Maurine V. Richardson, University of South Dakota, Vermillion

Elinor P. Ross, Tennessee Tech University, Cookeville

Vickie Ryan, Fairview School, Cullman, AL

Joye Coy Shaffer (retired), Literacy Volunteers of America, New Smyrna Beach, FL

Marilyn Skinner (retired), Kokomo Center Schools, IN

Jane Barber Smith, La Grange Elementary School, Poughquag, NY

John A. Smith, Wilson Elementary School, Logan, UT

Richard B. Speaker, Jr., University of New Orleans, LA

Anna Sumida, Kamehameha Elementary School, Honolulu, HI

Joan Tuttle, Marshall Simonds Elementary School, Burlington, MA

JoAnn Vandine, Carmichael Elementary School, Sierra Vista, AZ

Standards for the English Language Arts

Barbara J. Walker, Montana State University, Billings

Sarah Womble, Pulaski County Special School District, Little Rock, AR

Leanne Woodfill, Dean Morgan Junior High School, Casper, WY

IRA STATE COUNCIL PRESIDENTS AND COORDINATORS

Susan Abramson, President, 1993–1994, Finksburg, MD

Elizabeth Anderson, President, 1994–1995, Wichita, KS

Mary G. Anderson, President, 1993–1994, Elk City, OK

Sara Anderson, President, 1994–1995, Gladstone, MO

June Atkins, Coordinator, 1993–1996, Helena, MT

Paula J. Bailey, President, 1994–1995, Edmond, OK

Elizabeth M. Baker, Coordinator, 1993–1996, Columbia, MO

Lynne Z. Ball, President, 1994–1995, Boise, ID

Lucille Bartolomo, Coordinator, 1993–1994, West Simsbury, CT

Rose Ann Beason, President, 1995–1996, Neptune Beach, FL

Ed Becker, Coordinator, 1993–1994, Enterprise, KS

Stewart Behling, President, 1995–1996, Ferron, UT

Sherry G. Belk, President, 1993–1994, Monroe, NC

T. J. Betenbough, President, 1994–1995, Silver City, NM

Janice Lake Betts, President, 1993–1994, Petersburg, NJ

Kathryn A. Biggins, Coordinator, 1993–1996, North Scituate, RI

Gerry Bohning, President, 1993–1994, Ft. Lauderdale, FL

Elizabeth J. Bowers, Coordinator, 1993–1996, Rapid City, SD

Phyllis C. Brady, President, 1993–1994, Minneapolis, MN

Jo Anne Bryant, Coordinator, 1993–1996, Prattville, AL

Benita Buckles, President, 1993–1994, Elizabethtown, KY

Susan Fleming Buescher, President, 1995–1996, McCall, ID

Sandra E. Burgess, President, 1995–1996, San Antonio, TX

Janet A. Busboom, President, 1993–1994, Macon, GA

Oweita Calvert, President, 1995–1996, Cheyenne, OK

Jan Carlson, Coordinator, 1993–1996, Formoso, KS

Jacquie J. Casati, President, 1995–1996, Anchorage, AK

Jeanne G. Cheek, President, 1993–1994, Monroe City, MO

Roseine Church, President, 1993–1994, Cheyenne, WY

Sally W. Clark, President, 1994–1995, Marietta, GA

Tanna M. Clark, President, 1993–1994, Hot Springs National, AR

Donna M. Clause, Coordinator, 1993–1996, Long Branch, NJ

Betty Clifton, Coordinator, 1993–1996, Oklahoma City, OK

Ward Andrew Cockrum, President, 1994–1995, Sedona, AZ

Judy L. Cohen, President, 1994–1995, Highland Park, NJ

Donald E. Collins, Coordinator, 1993–1996, Fairfax, VT

Susan L. Collins, President, 1994–1995, Fairfax, VT

Clyde G. Colwell, President, 1993–1994, Norfolk, VA

Jacqueline C. Comas, President, 1994–1995, Gainesville, FL

Patsy J. Conner, President, 1994–1995, Sheridan, WY

Lois K. Cook, President, 1994–1995, Walpole, MA

Paula Costello, President, 1994–1995, N. Tonawanda, NY

Phyllis Y. Coulter, President, 1995–1996, Harrisonburg, VA

Elizabeth Cronemeyer, President, 1995–1996, Lawrence, KS

Joanne Cunard, Coordinator, 1993–1996, West Hartford, CT

Doris Walker Dalhouse, President, 1994–1995, Moorhead, MN

Cathy C. Davis, President, 1994–1995, Austin, TX

Thelma A. Davis, President, 1994–1995, Las Vegas, NV

Jean F. de Tarnowsky, President, 1995–1996, North Scituate, RI

Amy A. DeLucia, President, 1995–1996, Waterbury, CT

Marc A. Devenney, President, 1993–1994, Columbus, MS

Lawrence R. DeVoogd, President, 1994–1995, Muskegon, MI

Sharon A. Diaz, President, 1994–1995, Clarksburg, WV

Jean E. Doll, Coordinator, 1993–1994, Lancaster, PA

Dorothy F. Earle, President, 1995–1996, Salem, MA

Kathie J. Elder, President, 1995–1996, Helena, MT

Sherry M. Erwin, President, 1995–1996, Elko, NV

Nancy Jane Feeney, President, 1994–1995, Bel Air, MD

Joan Fingon, President, 1993–1994, Rutland, VT

Marsha Fisher, President, 1995–1996, Americus, GA

Carolyn J. Foster, President, 1995–1996, Portales, NM

Vincent P. Fouchi, President, 1994–1995, Metairie, LA

Susan M. Fowler, President, 1993–1996, Newport, OR

Marcella R. Frevert, President, 1993–1994, Emmetsburg, IA

Linda S. Fuller, Coordinator, 1993–1996, Schaumburg, IL

Marilyn C. Funes, President, 1995–1996, Staten Island, NY

Judith F. Galbert, President, 1995–1996, Fishers, IN

Cheryl B. Garner, President, 1993–1994, Ruston, LA

Gail Y. Gayeski, Coordinator, 1993–1996, Forty Fort, PA

Janis K. George, President, 1993–1994, Chattaroy, WA

Marguerite K. Gillis, Coordinator, 1993–1996, Buda, TX

Susan L. Gilmore, President, 1995–1996, Dover, DE

Wanda J. Glasshoff, President, 1993–1994, Gretna, NE

Cathy Goslin, Coordinator, 1993–1994, Stillwater, ME

Lannie R. Griffeth, President, 1994–1995, York, SC

Mary Jean Grimes, President, 1995–1996, Chehalis, WA

Kathleen A. Hall, President, 1995–1996, Kansas City, MO

Susan K. Hanks, President, 1994–1995, Normal, IL

Susan L. Hanson, Coordinator, 1993–1996, Juneau, AK

Dee Hayes, Coordinator, 1993–1994, Marne, MI

Kathy S. Neal Headley, President, 1993–1994, Clemson, SC

Elaine M. Healy, Coordinator, 1993–1996, Las Vegas, NV

Patricia B. Henry, Coordinator, 1993–1996, Casper, WY

Luann Hermreck, President, 1993–1994, Merriam, KS

Arlene Hett, President, 1993–1994, Great Falls, MT

Dennis C. Hickey, Coordinator, 1993–1996, Albany, OR

Jeff Hildreth, President, 1995–1996, De Kalb, IL

Joyce Hinman, Coordinator, 1993–1996, Bismarck, ND

Dianne M. Hoffman, President, 1995–1996, Reisterstown, MD

Ruby Hopwood, President, 1993–1994, Boardman, OH

Frances E. Horton, President, 1995–1996, Huntington, WV

Marilyn Howard, Coordinator, 1993–1996, Moscow, ID

Jill P. Hughes, President, 1995–1996, Utica, KY

Leslie A. Hume, Coordinator, 1993–1994, Smyrna, DE

Susan K. Imig, President, 1994–1995, Goehner, NE

Peggy Isakson, President, 1993–1994, Longmont, CO

Eren Johnson, Coordinator, 1993–1994, Woodlands, TX

Kathleen Stumpf Jongsma, President, 1993–1994, San Antonio, TX

Virginia W. Juettner, President, 1994–1995, Chugiak, AK

Lucille M. Keuntjes, President, 1994–1995, Wisconsin Rapids, WI

Adria F. Klein, President, 1995–1996, Redlands, CA

Beverly J. Klug, President, 1993–1994, Pocatello, ID

Barbara R. Kruse, President, 1994–1995, Loveland, CO

Helen Ladner, President, 1993–1994, Rapid City, SD

Roberta J. Laird, President, 1993–1994, Clarion, PA

Janet C. Langlois, President, 1995–1996, Baton Rouge, LA

Diane L. Larson, Coordinator, 1993–1996, Faribault, MN

Ann Laurimore, President, 1995–1996, Traverse City, MI

Nora Davenport Lawson, President, 1993–1994, Montgomery, AL

Judy Lavoie, Coordinator, 1993–1996, Gilford, NH

Marsha M. Lewis, Coordinator, 1993–1996, Kenansville, NC

Judy Lissman, President, 1995–1996, Torrington, WY

Marian Littman, President, 1993–1994, Oak Park, MI

Penny W. Love, President, 1993–1994, Manchester, NH

Norman C. Machart, President, 1994–1995, Valley City, ND

Barbara M. May, Coordinator, 1993–1996, Cedar Rapids, IA

Anita McClain, President, 1993–1994, Portland, OR

Coleen L. McClanahan, President, 1995–1996, Ames, IA

Faye C. McDonough, President, 1993–1994, Wiscasset, ME

Lois A. Meadows, President, 1993–1994, Parkersburg, WV

Penny K. Merriman, President, 1994–1995, Auburn, WA

Kristine M. Michell, President, 1995–1996, Green Bay, WI

Marilyn Miles, Coordinator, 1993–1996, Casa Mesa, CA

Arlene V. Militello, Coordinator, 1993–1994, North Kingstown, RI

Ann Millikan, Coordinator, 1993–1996, Kokomo, IN

Jocelyn Mokulehua, Coordinator, 1993–1996, Wahiawa, HI

Joanne K. Monroe, President, 1995–1996, Annandale, NJ

Karen Moore, President, 1994–1995, Placersville, CA

Joyce Morris, Coordinator, 1993–1996, Fairmont, WV

Mary H. Mosley, President, 1994–1995, Conway, AR

James Mullins, Coordinator, 1993–1994, Nokesville, VA

Carole Nagan, President, 1993–1994, Kodiak, AK

Linda Nishioka, Coordinator, 1993–1994, Mililani, HI

Patricia R. Nix, President, 1995–1996, Hoover, AL

Patricia C. Norman, Coordinator, 1993–1996, New Richmond, WI

Dale E. Norton, President, 1993–1994, Visalia, CA

Barbara A. Nourse, President, 1995–1996, Portsmouth, OH

Janet E. Nuckles, President, 1995–1996, Maplewood, MN

Julia Olive, President, 1995–1996, Chattanooga, TN

Rebecca L. Olness, President, 1993–1996, Kent, WA

Lillian L. Panchhi, Coordinator, 1993–1994, Reno, NV

Sharon Papineau, President, 1995–1996, Valley City, ND

Mary A. Parrish, President, 1994–1995, Alexandria, VA

Judy Poe, President, 1994–1995, East Liverpool, OH

Nancy J. Port, President, 1994–1995, Nevada, IA

Richard E. Potts, President, 1994–1995, Memphis, TN

Connie M. Pribbeno, President, 1995–1996, Imperial, NE

Dixie D. Pryor, President, 1994–1995, North Webster, IN

Ethna R. Reid, Coordinator, 1993–1994, Salt Lake City, UT

D. Ray Reutzel, Coordinator, 1993–1996, Provo, UT

G. Veloy Richards, President, 1993–1995, Farmington, UT

Marilyn Ridenhower, President, 1993–1994, Dickinson, ND

E. Jean Roberts, President, 1994–1995, Richmond, KY

Jean M. Roberts, Coordinator, 1993–1996, Superior, CO

Christine Roderick, President, 1995–1996, Gilford, NH

George E. Rusnak, President, 1995–1996, Swanton, VT

Vickie L. Ryan, President, 1994–1995, Cullman, AL

Norman S. Sam, President, 1993–1994, Coordinator, 1994–1996, Casa Grande, AZ

Susan Sandler, President, 1995–1996, Readfield, ME

Grace P. Sawyer, President, 1994–1995, Coordinator, 1995–1996, N. Whitefield, ME

Ronald J. Scherry, President, 1994–1995, Ballantine, MT

Bonnie L. Schmeltz, Coordinator, 1993–1996, Laurel, MD

Paula Schoenfelder, President, 1993–1994, Batavia, IL

Cynthia Seastrong, President, 1994–1995, Bridgeport, CT

Judith Shively, President, 1993–1994, Torrington, CT

Nancy Short, Coordinator, 1993–1996, Marion, OH

Martha A. Simpson, President, 1995–1996, Alexander, AR

Debra A. Sinclair, President, 1994–1995, Vermillion, SD

Barbara J. Singleton, Coordinator, 1993–1996, Ocean Springs, MS

Mary Ellen Skidmore, President, 1994–1995, Whispering Pines, NC

Darlene Skrdlant, Coordinator, 1993–1996, Bladen, NE

Jane Barber Smith, President, 1993–1994, Poughquag, NY

Sharon Smith, President, 1994–1995, Concord, NH

Hoyte Snow, Coordinator, 1993–1996, Brentwood, TN

Patricia A. Sowls, President, 1993–1994, New London, WI

Theodosia S. Spewock, President, 1995–1996, Hollidaysburg, PA

Peggy G. Stephenson, Coordinator, 1993–1996, Arlington, VA

Vicki C. Sterling, President, 1993–1996, Madison, SD

Sylvia M. Stevens, Coordinator, 1993–1996, President, 1993–1994, Dover, DE

Joan C. Stevenson, Coordinator, 1993–1996, Rock Hill, SC

Alice S. Stovall, Coordinator, 1993–1996, North Little Rock, AR

Madeleine D. St. Romain, Coordinator, 1993–1996, Stone Mountain, GA

JoAnn G. Sugden, President, 1994–1995, Woonsocket, RI

Constance Sullivan, President, 1993–1994, Middletown, RI

Ellen Supran, Coordinator, 1993–1996, Miami, FL

Ronald K. Sutherland, President, 1995–1996, Grand Junction, CO

Melinda S. Swain, Coordinator, 1993–1996, Gallup, NM

Philip Talbert, President, 1993–1994, Greenfield, IN

Dora D. Tartar, President, 1994–1995, Kunkletown, PA

Teresa F. Taylor, President, 1995–1996, Turbeville, SC

Dana G. Thames, President, 1994–1996, Petal, MS

Nancy Hunter Todd, Coordinator, 1993–1994, Louisville, KY

Rebecca B. Tonietti, Coordinator, 1993–1996, Glendale, KY

Frances M. Troxler, Coordinator, 1993–1996, Gramercy, LA

E. Jean Tucker, President, 1994–1995, Newark, DE

Joan L. Tuttle, President, 1993–1994, Woburn, MA

Marge R. Vallejos, President, 1993–1994, Las Vegas, NM

Kerry C. Vath, President, 1995–1996, Tucson, AZ

Brad L. Walker, President, 1995–1996, Wilmington, NC

Diane A. Walworth, President, 1994–1995, The Dalles, OR

Lillian Ward, President, 1993–1994, Gallatin, TN

Joan Warnaar, Coordinator, 1993–1996, Muskegon, MI

John R. Watkins, Jr., Coordinator, 1993–1996, Binghamton, NY

Nancy A. Zamierowski, Coordinator, 1993–1996, Arlington, MA

IRA REVIEWERS REPRESENTING LITERACY ORGANIZATIONS (Invited to review)

Martha Abbott, Fairfax County Public Schools, Falls Church, VA

Donna Alvermann, National Reading Research Center, University of Georgia, Athens

Gordon Ambach, Council of Chief State School Officers, Washington, DC

Lorraine Amico, Governors Association, Washington, DC

Richard C. Anderson, Center for the Study of Reading, University of Illinois at Urbana-Champaign

Arthur Applebee, National Research Center on Literature Teaching and Learning, SUNY, Albany

John Auchter, American Council on Education, Washington, DC

Richard Bagin, National School Public Relations Association, Arlington, VA

Peggy Barber, American Library Association, Chicago, IL

Patte Barth, Council for Basic Education, Washington, DC

David Bayless, Bayless and Associates, Research Triangle Park, NC

Michael Beck, Beck Evaluation and Testing Association, Pleasantville, NY

Kate Blossom, National Research Center on Literature Teaching and Learning, SUNY, Albany

Mary Lyn Bourque, National Assessment Governing Board, Washington, DC

Margaret Branson, Center for Civic Education, Calabasas, CA

Joan L. Buttram, Research for Better Schools, Philadelphia, PA

Sydell T. Carlton, Educational Testing Service, Princeton, NJ

Don Cartensen, American College Testing Program, Iowa City, IA

Charles Cascio, National Board of Professional Teaching Standards, Washington, DC

Micki Clemens, Singleton Education Centre, Burlington, ON

John Y. Cole, Center for the Book, Washington, DC

Joann Crandall, National Clearinghouse on Literature, Washington, DC

Brian Curry, Association for Supervision and Curriculum Development, Alexandria, VA

Glen W. Cutlip, National Education Association, Washington, DC

Kitty Dalton, Center for Early Adolescence, University of North Carolina, Carrboro

Stephanie Dalton, National Cultural Diversity Center, University of California, Santa Cruz

Anthony DeSouza, National Geographic Society, Washington, DC

Thomas Dickinson, National Middle School Association, Columbus, OH

John Dilworth, The Psychological Corporation, San Antonio, TX

Timothy Dyer, National Association of Secondary School Principals, Reston, VA

Lorraine Edmo, National Indian Education Association, Washington, DC

Sarah Freedman, National Center for the Study of Writing and Literacy, University of California, Berkeley

Mike Friedman, FairTest Examiner, Cambridge, MA

Lorraine Gaire, Educational Testing Service, Princeton, NJ

James Gates, National Council of Teachers of Mathematics, Reston, VA

Joel Gomez, National Association for Bilingual Education, Washington, DC

Gilbert Grovenor, National Geographic Society, Washington, DC

John Guthrie, National Reading Research Center, University of Maryland, College Park

Marilyn Hala, National Council of Teachers of Mathematics, Reston, VA

David Haynes, National Board for Professional Teaching Standards, Washington, DC

Joan Heman, Center for Research on Evaluation, Standards, and Student Testing, UCLA

Lois Karl, National Council of Teachers of Mathematics, Reston, VA

Nancy Katins, Educational Testing Service, Princeton, NJ

Stanley Katz, American Council of Learned Societies, New York, NY

Ernest Kimmel, Educational Testing Service, Princeton, NJ

Martharose Laffey, National Council for the Social Studies, Washington, DC

Linda Lange, Research for Better Schools, Philadelphia, PA

Julia Lara, Council for Chief State Schools Officers, Washington, DC

John Mahlmann, Music Educators National Conference, Reston, VA

Gary Marx, American Association of School Administrators, Arlington, VA

Lynn McFarlane, Center for Policy Research, New Brunswick, NJ

Mark Molli, Center for Civic Education, Washington, DC

Monty Neill, National Center for Fair and Open Testing, Cambridge, MA

Judith Olson-Fallon, Case Western Reserve University, Cleveland, OH

John O'Neil, Association for Supervision and Curriculum Development, Alexandria, VA

Jean Osborn, Center for the Study of Reading, University of Illinois at Urbana-Champaign

P. David Pearson, Formerly: Center for the Study of Reading, University of Illinois at Urbana-Champaign; Now: Michigan State University, East Lansing

Joy Peyton, Center for Applied Linguistics, Washington, DC

Andy Plattner, National Center on Education and the Economy, Washington, DC

George Powell, Educational Testing Service, Evanston, IL

Charles Quigley, Center for Civic Education, Calabasas, CA

Paula Quint, Children's Book Council, New York, NY

Allen A. Raymond, Teaching K–8, Norwalk, CT

David Reiderman, Children's Book Council, New York, NY

Marie Robinson, National Association of Elementary School Principals, Alexandria, VA

Bella Rosenberg, American Federation of Teachers, Washington, DC

Herb Salinger, American Association of School Personnel, Sacramento, CA

Samuel Sava, National Association of Elementary School Principals, Alexandria, VA

C. Edward Scebold, American Council of Teachers, Yonkers, NY

James Shriner, University of Minnesota, Minneapolis

Jay Smink, National Dropout Prevention Center, Atlanta, GA

Carol Smith, American Association of Colleges for Teacher Education, Washington, DC

Duane Smith, Center for Civic Education, Calabasas, CA

Pat Spahr, National Association for the Education of Young Children, Washington, DC

Willa Spicer, South Brunswick Public Schools, Monmouth Junction, NJ

Sandra G. Spooner, Cambridge Public Schools, MA

Don I. Tharpe, Association of School Business Officers, Reston, VA

Daniel Wagner, National Center on Adult Literacy, University of Pennsylvania, Philadelphia

Judy Wagner, Ohio State University, Columbus

Judith Walter, Association for Supervision and Curriculum Development, Alexandria, VA

Ruth Wattenberg, American Federation of Teachers, Washington, DC

Ann Weeks, American Association of School Librarians, Chicago, IL

Kathryn Whitfill, National PTA, Chicago, IL

Andrea Whittaker, Far West Laboratory, San Francisco, CA

Judy Young, National Association of State Personnel Executives, Reston, VA

REPRESENTATIVES OF STATE DEPARTMENTS OF EDUCATION AND STATE READING SPECIALISTS (Invited to review)

Bill Abrams, Department of Education, Carson City, NV

Herman M. Aizawa, State Department of Education, Honolulu, HI

Elizabeth Alfred, Nebraska Department of Education, Lincoln, NE

Nancy C. Andrews, Department of Education, Augusta, ME

Robert V. Antonucci, Department of Education, Malden, MA

Raymond G. Arveson, Department of Education, Baton Rouge, LA

June Atkins, Office of Public Instruction, Helena, MT

Paula Bailey, Monroney Junior High School, Midwest City, OK

Fred Bannister, Office of Public Instruction, Olympia, WA

JoEtta Barnett, Department of Education, Columbia, SC

Robert E. Bartman, Department of Elementary and Secondary Education, Jefferson City, MO

Scott W. Bean, State Office of Education, Salt Lake City, UT

Adelaida Bellin, Guam Department of Education, Agana, Guam

John T. Benson, State Department of Education, Madison, WI

Beth Berghoff, Indiana Department of Education, Indianapolis

Susan Carey Biggam, Department of Education, Montpelier, VT

Judith A. Billings, State Department of Public Instruction, Olympia, WA

Clarence Bina, State Department of Public Instruction, Bismarck, ND

C. Diane Bishop, State Department of Education, Phoenix, AZ

Diane Bloom, New Jersey Department of Education, Trenton

John Bonaiuto, State Department of Education, Pierre, SD

William C. Bosher, Jr., State Department of Education, Richmond, VA

Thomas C. Boysen, State Department of Education, Frankfort, KY

Kenneth Bradford, Department of Education, Richmond, VA

Mary Brandt, State Department of Education, Honolulu, HI

Frank T. Brogan, State Department of Education, Tallahassee, FL

Carol Brown, Ohio Department of Education, Columbus

Tom Burnham, State Department of Education, Jackson, MS

Donald M. Carroll, State Department of Education, Harrisburg, PA

Betty Castor, State Department of Education, Tallahassee, FL

Judy Catchpole, State Department of Education, Cheyenne, WY

James E. Cheek, State Department of Education, Charlotte Amalie, VI

Mitchell Chester, State Department of Education, Hartford, CT

Doug Christensen, State Department of Education, Lincoln, NE

Mary Beth Clark, Utah State Department of Education, Salt Lake City

Wilmer S. Cody, State Department of Education, Frankfort, KY

Trudy Collier, Maryland Department of Education, Baltimore

Jeanne Wells Cook, Mississippi Department of Education, Jackson

Karen Costello, State Department of Education, Hartford, CT

Gerald Covey, State Department of Education, Juneau, AK

Cris Crissman, Department of Public Instruction, Raleigh, NC

Mary Crovo, Washington, DC

Catherine Davis, Texas Education Agency, Austin

William Dawson, State Department of Education, Sacramento, CA

Dale M. Dennis, State Department of Education, Topeka, KS

Charlotte Diffendale, Rhode Island Department of Education, Providence

Imogene Draper, Roanoke, VA

Lee Droegemueller, State Department of Education, Topeka, KS

Delaine Eastin, State Department of Education, Sacramento, CA

Lois Easton, Arizona Department of Education, Phoenix

Hilda Edwards, Department of Education, Columbus, OH

Burton Elliott, State Department of Education, Little Rock, AR

Arthur Ellis, State Department of Education, Lansing, MI

Judith Entwife, Alaska Department of Education, Juneau

Bob Etheridge, State Department of Education, Raleigh, NC

Jerry Evans, State Department of Education, Boise, ID

Victor R. Fajardo, State Department of Education, San Juan, Puerto Rico

Vincent Ferrandino, State Department of Education, Hartford, CT

Rex Filmer, Nebraska Department of Education, Lincoln

L. R. Fischer, State Department of Education, Albany, NY

Mary Lee Fitzgerald, State Department of Education, Trenton, NJ

Bernard Floriani, Department of Public Instruction, Dover, DE

Pascal D. Forgione, Jr., State Department of Public Instruction, Dover, DE

Anne C. Fox, State Department of Education, Boise, ID

Michael W. Frye, State Department of Education, Raleigh, NC

Sandy Garrett, State Department of Education, Oklahoma City, OK

Judy Gilbert, Eagle Rock School, Estes Park, CO

John M. Goff, State Department of Education, Columbus, OH

Claudette Goss, Oklahoma Department of Education, Oklahoma City

Lisa Graham, State Department of Education, Phoenix, AZ

Nancy S. Grasmick, State Department of Education, Baltimore, MD

Alton L. Greenfield, Department of Education, St. Paul, MN

Dennis Gribbs, Department of Education, Pierre, SD

Herbert Grover, State Department of Education, Madison, WI

Jan Cladouhos Hahn, Montana Department of Education, Helena

Bill Hammond, Georgia Department of Education, Atlanta

Richard Harmston, Utah Department of Education, Salt Lake City

Cindi M. Heuts, Department of Public Instruction, Raleigh, NC

Geof Hewitt, Vermont Department of Education, Montpelier

Eugene W. Hickok, State Department of Education, Harrisburg, PA

Lynette Hill, Idaho Department of Education, Boise

Shirley J. Holloway, Department of Education, Juneau, AK

Judy Hood, Michigan Department of Education, Lansing

Juanita Hoskyn, Arkansas Department of Education, Little Rock

Betty Johnson, Indiana Department of Education, Indianapolis

Fred Johnson, Georgia Department of Education, Atlanta

Lory Johnson, Department of Education, Des Moines, IA

Barbara Kapinus, Council of Chief State School Officers, Washington, DC

Jacqueline Karbon, Wisconsin Department of Public Instruction, Madison

Nancy Keenan, State Office of Public Instruction, Helena, MT

Elizabeth M. King, Department of Education, Salem, OR

Lloyd Kjorness, Department of Education, Cheyenne, WY

Leo F. Klagholz, State Department of Education, Trenton, NJ

Diane Kubinski, State Department of Education, Trenton, NJ

Ellen Last, Wisconsin Department of Education, Madison

Robert Leininger, State Department of Education, Springfield, IL

Nancy Leinius, Wyoming Department of Education, Cheyenne

William Lepley, State Department of Education, Des Moines, IA

Nancy Livingston, Brigham Young University, Provo, UT

Joseph Lutjeharms, State Department of Education, Lincoln, NE

Gene Mammenga, State Department of Education, St. Paul, MN

Jacqueline Marino, New York State Department of Education, Albany

Henry R. Marockie, State Department of Education, Charleston, WV

Charles H. Marston, State Department of Education, Concord, MA

Leo G. Martin, Maine Department of Education, Augusta

Steve McAliley, Alabama Department of Education, Montgomery

Judy McCoy, Hawaii Department of Education, Honolulu

Peter McWalters, State Department of Education, Providence, RI

John L. Meehan, Department of Education, Harrisburg, PA

Lynn Meeks, State Department of Education, Boise, ID

Lionel R. Meno, State Department of Education, Austin, TX

Richard P. Mills, State Department of Education, Albany, NY

Warren R. Mitchell (retired), State Department of Education, Montgomery, AL

Alan D. Morgan, State Department of Education, Santa Fe, NM

Mike Moses, Texas Education Agency, Austin

Wayne L. Mowatt, State Department of Education, Augusta, ME

Barbara S. Nielsen, State Department of Education, Columbia, SC

Leila Norris, Department of Public Instruction, Bismarck, ND

Charlotte O'Brien, Missouri Department of Education, Jefferson City

Diana Ohman, State Department of Education, Cheyenne, WY

Alan Olds, Colorado Department of Education, Denver

Sharon O'Neal, Texas Education Agency, Austin

Dennis Parker, California Department of Education, Sacramento

Eugene Paslov, State Department of Education, Carson City, NV

Alberta Patch-Slegaitis, New York State Education Department, Albany

Norma Paulus, State Department of Education, Salem, OR

Mary Pautsch, Department of Education, KS

Mary L. Peterson, State Department of Education, Carson City, NV

Sheila Potter, Department of Education, Lansing, MI

Jo Prather, Mississippi Department of Education, Jackson

Katherine Pugh, Tennessee Department of Education, Nashville

Pat Rael, State Department of Education, Santa Fe, NM

William T. Randall, State Department of Education, Denver, CO

Suellen K. Reed, State Department of Education, Indianapolis, IN

Lawrence Richard, Texas Education Agency, Austin

Edward Richardson, State Department of Education, Montgomery, AL

Susan Richardson, State Board of Education, Springfield, IL

Marcia L. Rieder, McDougal Littell, Houghton Mifflin Company, Evanston, IL

Mel Riggs, Kansas Department of Education, Topeka

Juan J. Rodriguez, Department of Education, Hato Rey, Puerto Rico

Werner Rogers, State Department of Education, Atlanta, GA

Linda Romero, State Department of Education, Santa Fe, NM

John Rosario, Public School System, Northern Mariana Islands, Saipan, MP

Angela Rose, State Department of Education, Hartford, CT

Mary R. Rose, Department of Public Instruction, Raleigh, NC

Muriel Rosmann, Arizona State Department of Education, Phoenix

Ted Sanders, State Department of Education, Columbus, OH

Wayne G. Sanstead, State Department of Education, Bismarck, ND

Karon Schaack, Department of Education and Cultural Affairs, Pierre, SD

Robert Schiller, State Department of Education, Lansing, MI

Ann Schluter, State Department of Education, St. Paul, MN

Helen Schotanus, Department of Education, Concord, NH

Linda C. Schrenko, State Department of Education, Atlanta, GA

Theodore S. Sergi, State Department of Education, Hartford, CT

Diane Shock, State Department of Education, Worthington, OH

Cheryl Sigmon, South Carolina State Department of Education, Columbia

Diane K. Skiffington, Department of Education, Harrisburg, PA

Charles E. Smith, State Department of Education, Nashville, TN

Franklin L. Smith, District of Columbia Public Schools

Thomas Sobol, State Department of Education, Albany, NY

Joseph A. Spagnolo, State Board of Education, Springfield, IL

Judith Staten, Massachusetts Department of Education, Malden

Frederick M. Stillwill, State Department of Education, Des Moines, IA

Margaret Sullivan, New Hampshire Department of Education, Concord

Roland L. G. Taimanglo, Department of Education, Agana, Guam

Wayne Teague, State Department of Education, Montgomery, AL

Charles Toguchi, State Department of Education, Honolulu, HI

Elizabeth M. Twomey, State Department of Education, Concord, NH

Olga Vaughn, New York Education Department, Lancaster

Kathy Verille, School Improvement Unit, Phoenix, AZ

Kay Vincent, Kentucky Department of Education, Frankfort

Mary G. Wade, Bureau of School Improvement, Baton Rouge, LA

Florence Wakuya, State of Hawaii Department of Education, Honolulu

Jane Walters, State Department of Education, Nashville, TN

Susan Watt, Florida Department of Education, Tallahassee

David Westmoreland, Arkansas Department of Education, Little Rock

Mary White, District of Columbia Department of Education

Gene Wilhoit, State Department of Education, Little Rock, AR

Lea-Ruth C. Wilkins, Department of Education, Tallahassee, FL

Tish Wilson, Kentucky Department of Education, Frankfort

Barbara Wolfe, Oregon Department of Education, Salem

Katie Young, Louisiana Department of Education, Baton Rouge

Carla Zimerelli-Clifford, State Department of Education, Baltimore, MD

IRA REVIEWERS (Not listed elsewhere)

Ira E. Aaron, Athens, GA

Marcia Baghban, Queens College, CUNY, Flushing

Rose Ann Beason, Jacksonville, FL

David Berg, Public School 272, Carnarshi, NY

Cathy Biggins, N. Scituate, RI

Deanna Birdyshaw, Lansing, MI

Nancy L. Blackbill, Nazareth, PA

Phyllis Brazee, University of Maine, Orono

Marietta Catlin, Pierre, SD

Dorothy D. Chase, Community of Southern Nevada, Las Vegas

Fred Cheney, District 11, Colorado Springs, CO

Shirley Choo, Burnaby, British Columbia

Jo Cleland, Arizona State University West, Phoenix

Phyllis Y. Coulter, Eastern Mennonite University, Harrisonburg, VA

Bernice Cullinan, Sands Point, NY

JoAnne Dickey, Richmond, KY

Billie Enz, Arizona State University, Tempe

Marie H. Erwine, Pringle, PA

Mary Beth Fletcher, Lexington, MA

James Flood, San Diego State University, CA

Nancy W. Gammon, Harris-Stowe State College, St. Louis, MO

Julianne B. Y. Gehman, New Holland, PA

Lorraine Gerhart, Oconomowoc, WI

Evelyn Guentzel, Austin, MN

Kim Harper-Given, Halifax, Nova Scotia

Susan Harris-Sharples, Wheelock College, Boston, MA

Franklin L. Herrington, Jacksonville, FL

Sally Hilldruys, Fredricksburg, VA

Don Hillyard, Evansville, IN

Verna Hines, Big Walnut High School, Sunbury, OH

Joyce Hinman, Bismarck, ND

Janci Hurt, Winter Haven, FL

Will Johnson, Howard University, Washington, DC

Mary Watson Jones, Albany, GA

Kathryn George Kuhlman, Truman State University, Kirksville, MO

Brenda Lawson, Woodward Elementary School, Woodward, OK

Diane Levin, Language Arts Consultant, Sacramento, CA

James Lindon, Tuscarawas Valley High School, Zoarville, OH

Joye A. Lucas, Moses Lake, WA

Caryl Lyons, American College Testing, Iowa City, IA

Susan Malaska, Shelby City Schools, OH

Martha Maxwell, MM Associates, Kensington, MD

Donald McFeely, IRA Professional Development Associate, Indiana, PA

Marie S. Melican, Medford, MA

Max Miller, Glen Burnie, MD

James Mosenthal, University of Vermont, Burlington

Judith Olson-Fallon, Case Western Reserve University, Cleveland, OH

Nancy Padak, Kent State University, OH

Connie Palmer, Pierre, SD

Beth Parliament, Hazel, SD

Emily Miller Payne, Southwest Texas State University, San Marcos

Laurence Peters, Office of Education Research and Improvement, Washington, DC

Virginia S. Popper, Mercer University, Macon, GA

Karen Quinn, University of Illinois at Chicago

Fred Quinonez, Denver, CO

Robert Riordan, Cambridge Ridge & Latin School, MA

Andrea Rosenblatt, Miami, FL

Susan B. Schuster, Baltimore, MD

MaryJane Simpson, Mills, MA

Celia A. Stabile, Cranston, RI

Betty Steeds, Kent, WA

Jane Sullivan, Rowan College of New Jersey, Glassboro

Joyce Tanner, Kelowna, British Columbia

Martha Thurlow, University of Minnesota, Minneapolis

Margaret A. Valinsky, Pottsville, PA

Don Vescio, Wilkes University, Wilkes-Barre, PA

Sean Walmsley, University of Albany-SUNY

Pat Ward, District Reading Coordinator, New Castle, WY

Martha Wells, Emmetsburg, IA

Bruce Whitehead, School District #44, Missoula, MT

Beverly Wicinsky, Winneconne, WI

Ellen Witkowski, Academy of the Holy Name, Tampa, FL

John Wood, Kutztown University, PA

Marian Wulfot, Ontario, NY

Maureen Zientek, Holy Family School, St. Petersburg, FL

SESSIONS AT IRA CONVENTIONS AND REGIONAL CONFERENCES RELATED TO STANDARDS

National Standards for English Language Arts Education, Reading Research '93 Conference sponsored by IRA, San Antonio, TX, April 24, 1993.

Open Forum on the Standards Project for English Language Arts, IRA Annual Convention, San Antonio, TX, April 27, 1993.

The IRA/NCTE Partnership: The Standards Project for English Language Arts, IRA Annual Convention, San Antonio, TX, April 27, 1993.

Open Forum on Standards in English Language Arts, IRA Tenth Great Lakes Regional Reading Conference, Rosemont, IL, September 22, 1993.

Standards for the English Language Arts: An Emerging Reality, IRA 21st Southwest Regional Conference, Tulsa, OK, November 11, 1993.

English Language Arts Curriculum Standards, IRA 21st Southwest Regional Conference, Tulsa, OK, November 12, 1993.

Language Arts Standards State Representative Meeting, IRA 21st Southwest Regional Conference, Tulsa, OK, November 12, 1993.

IRA/NCTE National Standards for the English Language Arts: A Progress Report and Open Forum, IRA Fifteenth West Regional Conference, Reno, NV, February 25, 1994.

The Standards Project for English Language Arts: An Open Forum on Issues and Progress, IRA Annual Convention, Toronto, Ontario, May 11, 1994.

English Language Arts Forum, IRA 22nd Southwest Regional Conference, Little Rock, AR, November 18, 1994.

Education 2000: Standards and Assessments for World-Class Education in the English Language Arts, National Teleconference sponsored by International Reading Association, National Council of Teachers of English, Delaware State University, and Department of English, Purdue University, January 27, 1995.

Working Session: IRA Standards Project, IRA Annual Convention, Anaheim, CA, May 2, 1995.

Update on Standards: Efforts in the States, IRA Annual Convention, Anaheim, CA, May 3, 1995.

The IRA/NCTE English Language Arts Standards: What Do They Mean For You, Your Students, Your School? IRA 22nd Plains Regional Conference, Des Moines, IA, September 29, 1995.

Standards for English Language Arts: Update, Preview, and Plans, IRA Rocky Mountain Regional Conference, Billings, MT, October 19, 1995.

The IRA and NCTE Standards, First Combined IRA Regional Conference, Great Lakes and Southeast, Nashville, TN, November 11, 1995.

IRA AND NCTE CONSENSUS COMMITTEE

Victoria Purcell-Gates, Harvard Graduate School of Education, Cambridge, MA

Ramsay Selden, CCSO, Washington, DC

Dorothy Strickland, Rutgers University, New Brunswick, NJ

Carol Tateishi, Director, Bay Area Writing Project, Berkeley, CA

Douglas Vance, La Follette High School, Madison, WI

NCTE PRESIDENTS (During project duration)

Shirley Haley-James, 1990–1991, Georgia State University (retired)

James E. Davis, 1991–1992, Ohio University, Athens

Jesse Perry, 1992–1993, San Diego City Schools, CA (retired)

Janie Hydrick, 1993–1994, Entz Elementary School, Mesa, AZ

Miriam T. Chaplin, 1994–1995, Rutgers University, Camden, NJ

Beverly Ann Chin, 1995–1996, University of Montana, Missoula

NCTE EXECUTIVE COMMITTEE (1995–1996)

Beverly Ann Chin, *President;* University of Montana, Missoula

Carol Avery, *President-Elect;* Millersville, PA

Sheridan Blau, *Vice President;* University of California, Santa Barbara

Miriam T. Chaplin, *Past President;* Rutgers University, Camden, NJ

Judith M. Kelly, *Secondary Representative at Large;* Hine Junior High School, Washington, DC

Diane T. Orchard, *Elementary Representative at Large;* Lapeer Community Schools, MI

Greta D. Price, *Middle School Representative at Large;* Willowbrook Middle School, Compton, CA

Kathy G. Short, *Elementary Section Chair;* University of Arizona, Tucson

Joan Naomi Steiner, *Secondary Section Chair;* School District of Marinette, WI

Frank Madden, *College Section Chair;* Westchester Community College, Valhalla, NY

Betty C. Houser, *Secondary Section Associate Chair;* Belmond/Klemme High School, Belmond, IA

Kay Parks Bushman, *Secondary Section Associate Chair;* Ottawa High School, KS

Gail E. Hawisher, *College Section Assistant Chair;* University of Illinois at Urbana-Champaign

Lester Faigley, *CCCC Chair;* University of Texas at Austin

Carol Pope, *CEE Chair;* North Carolina State University, Raleigh

Donald L. Stephan, *CEL Chair;* Sidney High School, OH

IMMEDIATE PAST MEMBERS OF NCTE EXECUTIVE COMMITTEE

Janie Hydrick, *Past President;* Entz Elementary School, Mesa, AZ

Ruth Nathan, *Elementary Representative at Large;* Novato, CA

Willie Mae Crews, *Secondary Section Associate Chair;* Birmingham Public Schools, AL

James L. Hill, *College Section Chair;* Albany State College, GA

Jacqueline Jones Royster, *CCCC Chair;* Ohio State University, Columbus

NCTE STAFF

Miles Myers, Executive Director

Charles Suhor, Deputy Executive Director

Karen Smith, Associate Executive Director

Patricia Lambert Stock, Associate Executive Director

Katherine Hope, Associate Executive Director for Business

Jeanne Bohlen, Secretary to the Executive Director

Joellen Bryant, Staff Designer

Millie Davis, Director of Affiliate and Member Services

Maria Drees, Standards Project Associate

Lee Erwin, Editor

Mary Fortune, Standards Manager

Sandra Gibbs, Director of Special Programs

Michael Greer, Editor

Zarina M. Hock, Coordinator of Editorial Services

John Kelley, Administrative Assistant to the Executive Director

Margaret Lee, Staff Associate

Richard Long, Washington Representative

Cliff Maduzia, Director of Publication Services

Gwen McDuffy, Standards Project Secretary

Kathy Parham, Standards Coordinator

Rona S. Smith, Editor

Liz Spalding, Project Manager for Standards

Kent Williamson, Director of Marketing and Membership Development

CONSULTANTS

Lynn B. Jenkins, Northford, CT

Michael W. Kibby, State University of New York, Buffalo

John Mayher, New York University

Jean Osborn, Center for the Study of Reading, University of Illinois at Urbana-Champaign

Stephen Tchudi, University of Nevada, Reno

CONTRIBUTORS

Kathryn H. Au, University of Hawaii, Honolulu

Sheridan Blau, University of California, Santa Barbara

Sally Burgett, South Side Elementary School, Champaign, IL

Shirley Chambers, Auburndale Intermediate School, Corona, CA

Margaret Cusack, Ledgeview Elementary School, Clarence, NY

Dan Daniel, Parkersburg High School, WV

Millie Davis, NCTE, Urbana, IL

Marie Dionisio, Louis M. Klein Middle School, Harrison, NY

Pat Egenberger, Ustach Middle School, Modesto, CA

Douglas Felter, Union County Regional High School District #1, Clarke, NJ

Cynthia W. Joor, Harmony Hills Elementary School, NEISD, New Jersey Writing Project in Texas; San Antonio, TX

Michael Kibby, State University of New York, Buffalo

Callie R. Kingsbury, State College Area School District, State College, PA

Joy McCaleb, Upperman High School, Baxter, TN

Carol Santa, School District #5, Kalispell, MT

Susan Stires, Center for Teaching and Learning, Edgecomb, ME

Carol Tateishi, Bay Area Writing Project, Berkeley, CA

Susan Katz Weinberg, University of New Mexico, Albuquerque

NCTE ELEMENTARY SECTION STEERING COMMITTEE

Kathy G. Short, *Chair;* University of Arizona, Tucson

Carol Avery, Millersville, PA

Pat Cordeiro, Rhode Island College, Providence

Cora Lee Five, Edgewood School, Scarsdale, NY

Jerome Harste, Indiana University, Bloomington

Don Howard, Oak Park, IL

Donna Maxim, Center for Teaching and Learning, Edgecomb, ME

Regie Routman, Shaker Heights (Ohio) City School District

Yvonne Siu-Runyan, University of Northern Colorado, Greeley

Standards for the English Language Arts

Bill Newby, Shaker Heights High School, OH

Wanda Porter, Kamehameha Secondary School, Honolulu, HI

James Strickland, Slippery Rock University, PA

Henry Kiernan, *ex officio*, Editor, *English Leadership Quarterly;* West Morris Regional High School, Chester, NJ

NCTE CONFERENCE ON COLLEGE COMPOSITION AND COMMUNICATION (CCCC) EXECUTIVE COMMITTEE

Lester Faigley, *Chair;* University of Texas at Austin

Nell Ann Pickett, *Assistant Chair;* Hinds Community College, Raymond, MS

Cynthia L. Selfe, *Assistant Chair;* Michigan Technological University, Houghton

Jacqueline Jones Royster, *Past Chair;* Ohio State University, Columbus

Barbara Stout, *Secretary;* Montgomery College, Rockville, MD

Chris Anson, University of Minnesota, Minneapolis

Lilly Bay, Rockland Community College, Suffern, NY

Suzanne Benally, Western Interstate Commission for Higher Education, Boulder, CO

Don Bialostosky, Pennsylvania State University, University Park

Paul Bodmer, Bismarck State College, ND

Rebecca E. Burnett, Iowa State University, Ames

Kermit E. Campbell, University of Texas, Austin

Juanita Comfort, Old Dominion University, Norfolk, VA

JoEllen Coppersmith, Utah Valley State College, Orem

Peter Elbow, University of Hawaii, Honolulu

Theresa Enos, University of Arizona, Tucson

Richard Fulkerson, East Texas State University, Commerce

Paula F. Gillespie, Whitefish Bay, WI

Barbara Guilland, Big Bend Community College, Moses Lake, WA

Patricia Harkin, Purdue University, W. Lafayette, IN

Richard H. Haswell, Washington State University, Pullman

Deborah James, University of North Carolina, Asheville

Gesa E. Kirsch, Wayne State University, Detroit, MI

Dennis Kriewald, Laredo Community College, TX

LuMing Mao, Miami University, Oxford, OH

Beverly Moss, Ohio State University, Columbus

Elizabeth Nist, Anoka-Ramsey Community College, Coon Rapids, MN

Teresa M. Redd, Howard University, Washington, DC

Mark Reynolds, Jefferson Davis Community College, Brewton, AL

Nedra Reynolds, University of Rhode Island, Kingston

M. Elizabeth (Betsy) Sargent, Western Oregon State College, Monmouth

Marie Secor, Pennsylvania State University, University Park

C. Jan Swearingen, University of Texas, Arlington

Arthur Young, Clemson University, SC

Joseph Harris, *ex officio*, Editor, *College Composition and Communication;* University of Pittsburgh, PA

NCTE CONFERENCE ON ENGLISH EDUCATION (CEE) EXECUTIVE COMMITTEE

Carol Pope, *Chair;* North Carolina State University, Raleigh

Patricia Kelly, *Vice Chair;* Virginia Polytechnic Institute, Blacksburg

Richard Harmston, *Recording Secretary;* Utah State Office of Education, Salt Lake City

Susan Hynds, Syracuse University, NY

Rosalie Black Kiah, Norfolk State University, VA

Nancy McCracken, Kent State University, OH

Peter Medway, Carleton University, Ottawa, Ontario

Susan Ohanian, Charlotte, VT

Maria de la Luz Reyes, University of California

Tom Romano, Utah State University, Logan

Hephzibah Roskelly, University of North Carolina, Greensboro

Bonnie Sunstein, University of Iowa, Iowa City

Don Zancanella, University of New Mexico, Albuquerque

Miles Myers, *NCTE Staff Liaison;* Urbana, IL

NCTE COMMISSION DIRECTORS

Christine Kline, *Commission on Composition;* University of Puget Sound, Tacoma, WA

Kathleen Dudden Andrasick, *Commission on Curriculum;* University of Hawaii-Manoa

Roseann Dueñas Gonzalez, *Commission on Language;* University of Arizona, Tucson

Carol Jago, *Commission on Literature;* Santa Monica High School, CA

Lawrence B. Fuller, *Commission on Media;* Bloomsburg University, PA

Diane Stephens, *Commission on Reading;* University of Hawaii at Manoa

NCTE BLACK CAUCUS CHAIR

Keith Gilyard, Syracuse University, NY (CCCC Executive Committee)

NCTE LATINO CAUCUS CHAIRS

MaryCarmen E. Cruz, Cholla High School, Tucson, AZ

Cecilia Rodriguez Milanes, Indiana University of Pennsylvania

NCTE STANDARDS RETREAT PARTICIPANTS (July 1993 and July 1994)

Wendy Bishop, Florida State University, Tallahassee

Lil Brannon, State University of New York at Albany

Barbara Cambridge, Indiana University-Purdue University at Indianapolis

Linda Crafton, Northwestern University, Evanston, IL

James Davis, Ohio University, Athens

Lela DeToye, Southern Illinois University, Carbondale

Barbara Flores, California State University, San Bernardino

Anne Ruggles Gere, University of Michigan, Ann Arbor

Doris Ginn, Jackson State University, MS

Jacquelyn Harris, St. Louis Public Schools, MO

Betty Hart, University of Southern Indiana, Evansville

Frankey Jones, Brookwood Elementary School, Snellville, GA

Thomas Jones, Wyoming Valley West High School, Plymouth, PA

Willa Mae Kippes, Valley High School, Gilcrest, CO

William McBride, Colorado State University, Fort Collins

Ann McCallum, Fairfax County Public Schools, Annandale, VA

Kevin McHugh, Finneytown Junior/Senior High School, Cincinnati, OH

Mildred Miller, Laguna Beach High School, CA

Patricia Phelan, University of San Diego, CA

Helen Schwartz, Indiana University-Purdue University at Indianapolis

Connie Sears, Weatherford High School, OK

Consentine Thompson, Ballou High School, Washington, DC

Judith Wambu, Kean College of New Jersey

ASSEMBLY OF STATE COORDINATORS OF ENGLISH LANGUAGE ARTS (ASCELA)

Bill Abrams, Nevada Department of Education, Carson City

Amy Alday-Murray, Oregon Department of Education, Salem

Nancy Andrews, Maine Department of Education, Augusta

Adelaida Bellin, Guam Department of Education, Agana

Anne Bendixen, Michigan Department of Education, Lansing

Clarence Bina, North Dakota Department of Education, Bismarck

Dianne Bloom, New Jersey Department of Education, Trenton

Kenneth Bradford, Virginia Department of Education, Richmond

Carol Brown, Ohio Department of Education, Columbus

Mary Beth Clark, Utah State Office of Education, Salt Lake City

Jeanne Wells Cook, Mississippi Department of Education, Jackson

Karen Costello, Madison (Connecticut) School District

Charlotte Diffendale, Rhode Island Department of Education, Providence

Judith Entwife, Alaska Department of Education, Juneau

Rex Filmer, Nebraska Department of Education, Lincoln

Bernard Floriani, Delaware Department of Public Instruction, Dover

John Fortier, Wisconsin Department of Education, Madison

Mike Frye, North Carolina Department of Education, Raleigh

Judy Gilbert, Eagle Rock School, Estes Park, CO

Claudette Goss, Oklahoma Department of Education, Oklahoma City

Al Greenfield, Minnesota Department of Education, St. Paul

Mae Gundach, California Department of Education, Sacramento

Jan Cladouhos Hahn, Montana Department of Education, Helena

Richard Harmstron, Utah State Office of Education, Salt Lake City

Robert Harrison, West Virginia Department of Education, Charleston

Geoff Hewitt, Vermont Department of Education, Montpelier

Lynette Hill, Idaho Department of Education, Boise

Veronica Huller, Illinois State Board of Education, Springfield

Fred Johnson, Georgia Department of Education, Atlanta

Lory Nels Johnson, Iowa Department of Education, Des Moines

Barbara Kapinus, Council of Chief State School Officers, Washington, DC

Ellen Last, Wisconsin Department of Education, Madison

Nancy Leinius, Wyoming Department of Education, Cheyenne

Starr Lewis, Kentucky Department of Education, Frankfort

Kathleen Lindas, Wisconsin Department of Public Instruction, Madison

Jacqueline Marino, New York State Department of Education, Albany

Steve McAliley, Alabama Department of Education, Montgomery

Judy McCoy, Hawaii Department of Education, Honolulu

Charlotte O'Brien, Missouri Department of Education, Jefferson City

Alan Olds, Colorado Department of Education, Denver

Sharon O'Neal, Texas Education Agency, Austin

Dennis Parker, California Department of Education, Sacramento

Gayle Pauley, Washington Department of Education, Olympia

Sheila Potter, Michigan Department of Education, Lansing

Kathryne Pugh, Tennessee Department of Education, Nashville

Fred Quinonez, Colorado Department of Education, Denver

Beverly Reitsma, Indiana Department of Education, Indianapolis

Lawrence Richard, Texas Education Agency, Austin

Susan Richardson, Illinois State Board of Education, Springfield

Mel Riggs, Kansas Department of Education, Topeka

Linda Romaro, New Mexico Department of Education, Santa Fe

John Rosario, Public School System, Northern Mariana Islands, Saipan MP

Muriel Rosmann, Arizona Department of Education, Phoenix

Cheryl Sigmon, South Carolina Department of Education, Columbia

Diane Skiffington, Pennsylvania Department of Education, Harrisburg

Ruth Smith, South Dakota Department of Education, Pierre

Judith Staten, Massachusetts Department of Education, Malden

Margaret Sullivan, New Hampshire Department of Education, Concord

Peggy Taylor, Washington Department of Education, Olympia

Lanny van Allen, Texas Education Agency, Austin

Kay Warner, Kentucky Department of Education, Frankfort

Susan Watt, Florida Department of Education, Tallahassee

David Westmoreland, Arkansas Department of Education, Little Rock

Mary White, District of Columbia Department of Education

Barbara Wolfe, Oregon Department of Education, Salem

Katie Young, Louisiana Department of Education, Baton Rouge

Carla Zamerelli-Clifford, Maryland Department of Education, Baltimore

REVIEWERS FROM OTHER ORGANIZATIONS (*See also* NCTE Affiliate and Chartered Task Forces)

Roy Berko, Associate Director, Speech Communication Association, Annandale, VA

Shirley R. Crenshaw, Research & Training Associates, Inc., Overland Park, KS

Margaret M. Crisculoa, The Great Books Foundation, Chicago, IL

Robert C. Dixon, National Center to Improve the Tools of Educators, Olympia, WA

Marisa Farnum, Senior Examiner, Educational Testing Service, Princeton, NJ

Mary Fowles, Principal Measurement Specialist, Educational Testing Service, Princeton, NJ

Kenneth Ives, *Journal of the Simplified Spelling Society,* Chicago, IL

Pam Ladd, Kentucky Writing Program, Paducah

Gary Marx, Senior Associate Executive Director, American Association of School Administrators, Arlington, VA

Paul Ramsey, Vice President, Teaching and Learning Programs, Educational Testing Service, Princeton, NJ

David Russell, Iowa State University, Ames

William J. Starosta, Speech Communication Association, Howard University, Washington, DC

Julie Tallman, The American Association of School Librarians, University of Georgia

Connie Wolfe, Kentucky Middle School Association, Midway College

NCTE AFFILIATE AND CHARTERED TASK FORCES

Acadiana CTE Affiliate Task Force, New Iberia, LA

Alabama CTE Affiliate Task Force, Enterprise

Alaska State Writing Consortium, Juneau

Alverno College English Department, Milwaukee, WI

Amarillo ISD Language Arts Chartered Task Force, TX

AMS Communication Arts Department, Ardsley, NY

Archbishop Hannan High School English Department, Meraux, LA

Arizona ETA Affiliate Task Force, Glendale

Association of College Teachers of Alabama Affiliate Task Force, Montevallo

Audrey Cohen College, Department of Curriculum and Instruction, Mamaronech, NY

Ball State University Standards Project Task Force, Muncie, IN

Bay Area Writing Project, Berkeley, CA

Bellows Free Academy English Department, St. Albans, VT

Bismarck Teachers Applying Whole Language, ND

Byron C.U.S.D. #226 Whole Language Council, IL

Capital Area Writing Project, Middletown, PA

CEA Task Force #2, Dearborn, MI

Central California CTE Affiliate Task Force, San Francisco

Central Jersey Teachers Applying Whole Language, Princeton

Central VATE Affiliate Task Force, Richmond, VA

Chapter I, ECIA, Rosedale, MS

Chartered Task Force on Workplace Literacy, Great Lakes, IL

Clackamas High School English Department, Portland, OR

Coastal Area Teachers Applying Whole Language/Coastal Area Writing Project, Myrtle Beach, SC

Coastal Georgia Writing Project, Savannah

Cobb County Schools Secondary English Curriculum Committee, Marietta, GA

College English Association SPELA Task Force #3, Silver Spring, MD

College English Association SPELA Task Force #4, Fort Wayne, IN

Colorado LAS Affiliate Task Force, Arvada

Connecticut CTE Affiliate Task Force, Fairfield

Curriculum Study Commission, Napa, CA

Dade County CTE Affiliate Standards Task Force, Miami, FL

Dayton Language Arts Assessment Team, OH

DC CTE Affiliate Task Force, Washington

Denton Avenue School, New Hyde Park, NY

Driscoll Catholic High School English Department, Addison, IL

Dwight Elementary #232, IL

East Baton Rouge CTE Affiliate Task Force, LA

East End Teachers Applying Whole Language, Southampton, NY

East Hartford Public Schools, CT

East Tennessee CTE Affiliate Task Force, Maryville

Eastern Shore/Northern Neck VATE Affiliate Task Force, Eastville, VA

Ecole Connaught Community School, Regina, Saskatchewan

Education Development Center Task Force, Newton, MA

Education Trust-American Association for Higher Education, Washington, DC

Educators of Deaf/Hard-of-Hearing Students, Portland, OR

English Department of Bishop McDevitt High School, Harrisburg, PA

English Department, South Tredell High School, Statesville, NC

ETC Public Schools Task Force, Ramsay, MI

ETS Group for English & Verbal Ability, Princeton, NJ

Florida CTE (Commission on Blueprint 2000) Affiliate Task Force, Jacksonville

Florida CTE Affiliate Task Force, Orlando

Florida State University Task Force, Tallahassee

Forest Park Professional Study Group, East Northport, NY

Frameworks Grant Curriculum and Advisory Committee, Helena, MT

Gardiner Area High School English Department, ME

Georgia LA Supervisors Affiliate Task Force, Decatur

Grapevine-Colleyville Writing-Reading Cadre, Roanoke, TX

Greater Akron TELA Affiliate Task Force, OH

Greater Louisville EC Affiliate Task Force, KY

Greater St. Louis English Teachers Association, MO

Haddonfield Memorial High School, NJ

Hawkins Language Arts, Hattiesburg, MS

Hazelwood School District, Florissant, MO

High Expectations in Literacy, Greeley, CO

High Plains Task Force, Portales, NM

Holton High School English Teachers, KS

Holy Cross Area Schools, Portland, OR

Houston CTE Affiliate Task Force, Missouri City, TX

Humble Independent School District, TX

Idaho CTE Affiliate Task Force, Boise

Inland Northwest CTE, Moses Lake, WA

Inland Northwest CTE Affiliate Task Force, Odessa, WA

Iowa Writing Project, Cedar Rapids

Jackson Public School District, MS

Jersey City Implementation Team, NJ

Joint Task Force on Standards, Madison, WI

K–12 Language Arts, Longview, WA

Kentucky CTE/LA Affiliate Task Force, Paducah

Kiona-Benton Committee on Standard Practices in English, Benton City, WA

Lamar Cluster, Arlington, TX

Language Arts Committee Stage 1, Soldotna, AK

Language Arts Department of Southwest Missouri Affiliate Task Force, Springfield

Language Arts Standards Project of the Los Angeles Unified School District, CA

Ledgeview Network, Williamsville, NY

Leflore County School District Language Arts Task Force, Greenwood, MA

Lincoln Junior High Standards Team, Burns, OR

The Literacy Connection, Granville, OH

Logan High School English Standards Task Force, UT

Long Branch High School English Department, NJ

Louisiana CTE Affiliate Task Force, Alexandria

Loveland High School English Department, CO

Lowell Language Arts Committee, Waukesha, WI

Maine CELA Affiliate Task Force, Brunswick

Maryland LEA Supervisors' Network, Baltimore

Maryland Writing Project, Towson

Massachusetts CTE Affiliate Task Force, Arlington

McREL Group, Aurora, CO

Michigan CTE Region 1 Affiliate Task Force, Detroit

Michigan CTE Region 4 Affiliate Task Force, Waterford

Michigan CTE Region 8 Affiliate Task Force, Kalamazoo

Middle Tennessee Teachers Applying Whole Language, Nashville

Midlands Writing Project, Columbia, SC

Mid-Missouri Teachers Applying Whole Language Task Force for Language Arts Standards, Columbia

Minnesota CTE Affiliate Task Force, St. Paul

Mississippi CTE Affiliate Task Force, Jackson

Missoula County Public Schools, MT

Missouri ATE Affiliate Task Force, Columbia

Monroe County Teachers Exploring Language & Literacy, Trenton, MI

Montana ATELA Affiliate Task Force, Missoula

Montgomery County Public Schools, Rockville, MD

Mt. St. Mary Academy Language Arts Project, Kenmore, NY

Naperville School District #203 Literacy Committee, IL

Nashville CTE Affiliate Task Force, Hermitage, TN

National Center to Improve Practice: Using Technology & Media to Promote Language Arts Outcomes for Students with Disabilities, Newton, MA

National Computer Systems and Eden Prairie Community School System, MN

National Writing Project of Acadiana, Lafayette, LA

NCRE Task Force, Cambridge, MA

NCTE Commission on Literature, Pacific Palisades, CA

NCTE Commission on Media, Long Beach, CA

Nebraska ELAC Affiliate Task Force, Omaha

Nevada Department of Education, Carson City

Nevada State CTE Affiliate Task Force, Reno

New Hampshire Postsecondary Communications Task Force, Laconia

The New Jersey Writing Project in Texas, Spring, TX

New Mexico CTE Affiliate Task Force, Albuquerque

New Orleans Public Schools English Language Arts Task Force, LA

New River/Roanoke Valley VATE Affiliate Task Force, Salem, VA

New York State EC Affiliate Task Force, Garden City

Newark Board of Education, NJ

Newport News City Schools, VA

North Carolina ETA Affiliate Task Force, Cherryville

North Community High School English Department, Minneapolis, MN

North Dakota English Collaborative, Bismarck

North Eastern Section of Connecticut Task Force, Dayville

North Harris County CTE Affiliate Task Force, Houston, TX

North Scott Junior High School Task Force, Bettendorf, IA

North Shore School District 112, Highland Park, IL

Northern Arizona Task Force, Flagstaff

Northern VATE Affiliate Task Force, Annandale, VA

Northwest Educators of Deaf/Hard-of-Hearing Students, Vancouver, WA

Northwest Pennsylvania CTE, Edinboro

Northwestern Pennsylvania English Standards Task Force, Edinboro

Ohio CTELA Affiliate Task Force, Columbus

Ohio Regional Assessment Network, Beachwood

Oklahoma Language Arts Supervisors, Oklahoma City

Oklahoma State University Writing Project, Stillwater

Oregon CTE Affiliate Task Force, Corvallis

Parkway School District ELA Department, St. Louis, MO

PAWP/PENNLIT Standards Task Force, Kennett Square, PA

Pennsylvania Writing and Literature Projects, West Chester

Performance-Based Language Arts Reading Committee, Evergreen, CO

Philippine English Studies & Comparative Literature Association Affiliate Task Force, University of the Philippines, Quezon City

Pine Elementary, Michigan City, IN

Pine Tree Standards Project for English Language Arts, Longview, TX

Pinellas County CTE Affiliate Task Force, St. Petersburg, FL

Pleasant Valley School District, Brodheadsville, PA

Prince George's County Public Schools English Language Arts Department, Landover, MD

Prince William County Public Schools Task Force, Manassas, VA

Public Schools English Language Arts Committee, Lexington, MA

Quincy Public Schools English Language Arts Task Force, MA

Rabun Gap-Nacoochee, Rabun Gap, GA

Redwood CTE Affiliate Task Force, Fortuna, CA

Rhode Island CTE Affiliate Task Force, Providence

Rio Grande Valley Language Arts Coordinators, McAllen, TX

Rural Technical Assistance Center, Regions 6, 7, & 8, Portland, OR

San Antonio Literacy Network, TX

San Diego City Schools, CA

Santee-Wateree Writing Project, Columbia, SC

Scholastic Network English Standards On-Line Task Force, New York, NY

Secondary Language Arts (6–12) Curriculum Development Committee, Springfield, MO

Seekonk High School Language Arts Team, MA

Shelby-Memphis CTE Affiliate Task Force, Memphis, TN

Sheldon-Williams Collegiate English Department, Regina, Saskatchewan

Shenandoah Valley VATE Affiliate Task Force, Harrisonburg, VA

Shine Standards Task Force, Hershey, PA

South Brunswick Language Arts Standards Task Force, Monmouth Junction, NJ

Southeast Texas CTE Affiliate Task Force, Beaumont

Southeastern VATE Affiliate Task Force, Chesapeake, VA

Southern Nevada TELA Affiliate Task Force, Henderson

Southside VATE Affiliate Task Force, Farmville, VA

Southwestern VATE Affiliate Task Force, Pound, VA

Sparta English/Reading Department, NJ

St. James English Standards Team, MO

St. Vrain Valley Task Force, Longmont, CO

Standards Project Study Group, Overland Park, KS

State of Idaho Department of Education, Boise

Task Force #1, CEA, Houston, TX

Tennessee CTE Affiliate Task Force, Cookeville

Texas CTE Affiliate Task Force, Houston

Texas CTE Affiliate Task Force, Marshall

Thames English Language Arts Standards Task Force, Hattiesburg, MS

Theodore Roosevelt High School English Department, Kent, OH

Tremper Semantics, Tremper High School, Kenosha, WI

Tri-County Education Service Center, Channahon, IL

Tri-County, Tri-Racial Task Force (Hoke, Robeson, and Scotland Counties), Pembroke, NC

University of North Carolina at Charlotte Writing Project

Utah CTELA Affiliate Task Force, Salt Lake City

Valparaiso High School, IN

Virginia ATE Affiliate Task Force, Christiansburg

Virginia Department of Education, Richmond

Walker County Board of Education, Jasper, AL

Washington State CTE Affiliate Task Force, Longview

Wayne County High School, Jessup, GA

Wayne County High School English Task Force, Waynesboro, MS

West Tennessee CTE Affiliate Task Force, Oakfield

Western Massachusetts Writing Project, Amherst

Western Pennsylvania CTE Affiliate Task Force, Tarentum

Westside Community Schools, Omaha, NE

Willowbrook High School English Department, Morris, IL

Wilmington, MA, English/Language Arts

Wisconsin Assessment Consortium

Wood Oaks Junior High, Northbrook, IL

Wyoming ATE Affiliate Task Force, Cheyenne

Y.I.S.D. Pebble Hills School Task Force, El Paso, TX

NCTE CONVENTION AND CONFERENCE SESSIONS RELATED TO STANDARDS

The Role of State Agencies in Setting Standards, Curriculum, and Assessment, and How You Can Be Involved, sponsored by the Assembly of State Coordinators of English/Language Arts, NCTE Annual Convention, Louisville, KY, November 1992.

English Language Arts Standards: An Open Forum, NCTE Annual Convention, Louisville, KY, November 1992.

Academic Standards and the Right, NCTE Annual Convention, Louisville, KY, November 1992.

If NCTE Had Published Standards Like NCTM, What Would They Be? NCTE Annual Convention, Louisville, KY, November 1992.

The Discourse of Educating for Democracy: Toward Its Critical Reconstruction, NCTE Spring Conference, Richmond, VA, March 1993.

English Language Arts Standards: An Open Forum, NCTE Spring Conference, Richmond, VA, March 1993.

Standards for All, NCTE Annual Convention, Pittsburgh, PA, November 1993.

Who Will Control the English Classroom? A Forum on National Standards, NCTE Annual Convention, Pittsburgh, PA, November 1993.

Standards for English Language Arts in Democratic Cultures, NCTE Annual Convention, Pittsburgh, PA, November 1993.

National Standards: Questions of Equity, sponsored by the Committee on Racism and Bias in the Teaching of English, the Black Caucus, and the Latino Caucus, NCTE Annual Convention, Pittsburgh, PA, November 1993.

Standards! Standards! Standards! What Are They? Who Sets Them? NCTE Annual Convention, Pittsburgh, PA, November 1993.

Standards and Assessment, NCTE Annual Convention, Pittsburgh, PA, November 1993.

Standards, NCTE Annual Convention, Pittsburgh, PA, November 1993.

Setting Up Standards in England, NCTE Annual Convention, Pittsburgh, PA, November 1993.

Working Session on the Standards Project for English Language Arts, NCTE Annual Convention, Pittsburgh, PA, November 1993.

Authentic Assessment, NCTE Annual Convention, Pittsburgh, PA, November 1993.

Working Session on the Standards Project for English Language Arts, NCTE Annual Convention, Pittsburgh, PA, November 1993.

Standards Issues, presented by Brian Cox, University of Manchester, United Kingdom, NCTE Annual Convention, Pittsburgh, PA, November 1993.

Open Forum on the Standards Project for English Language Arts, NCTE Annual Convention, Pittsburgh, PA, November 1993.

Democratic Classrooms with "Standards"? sponsored by the Elementary Section, NCTE Spring Conference, Portland, OR, March 1994.

Open Forum on the Standards Project for English Language Arts, NCTE Spring Conference, Portland, OR, March 1994.

Working Session on the Standards Project for English Language Arts, NCTE Spring Conference, Portland, OR, March 1994.

Working Session on the Standards Project for English Language Arts, NCTE Annual Convention, Orlando, FL, November 1994.

College Section Forum: The Debate on National Standards, NCTE Annual Convention, Orlando, FL, November 1994.

Standards for English Language Arts: Project Update and Open Forum, NCTE Annual Convention, Orlando, FL, November 1994.

The Search for Standards and Common Sense in the Assessment of English Language Arts, sponsored by the Standing Committee on Testing and Evaluation, NCTE Annual Convention, Orlando, FL, November 1994.

English Standards, NCTE Annual Convention, Orlando, FL, November 1994.

Standards for Democratic Classrooms: A Grassroots Working Party, sponsored by the Conference on English Education, NCTE Spring Conference, Minneapolis, MN, March 1995.

Conversations about Humanities: What if I Love Humanities? What if I Write Poetry? Can Standards and Assessments Be Vehicles for Professional and Personal Growth? NCTE Spring Conference, Minneapolis, MN, March 1995.

Working Session on the Standards Project for English Language Arts, NCTE Spring Conference, Minneapolis, MN, March 1995.

A Report on Recent Attempts to Reform National Curriculum and Assessment in South Africa and the United Kingdom, sponsored by the International Assembly, NCTE Spring Conference, Minneapolis, MN, March 1995.

Why CCCC Should Participate in the Standards Project, CCCC Annual Convention, Washington, DC, March 1995.

National Standards for the English Language Arts in the USA, NCTE International Conference: Reconstructing Language and Learning for the 21st Century, New York, NY, July 1995.

What Parents and School Boards Should Look for in the NCTE/IRA Content Standards, NCTE Annual Convention, San Diego, CA, November 1995.

Update on the NCTE/IRA Content Standards, NCTE Annual Convention, San Diego, CA, November 1995.

NCTE/IRA Content Standards: From Concept to Classroom, NCTE Annual Convention, San Diego, CA, November 1995.

How States and Local Districts Can Use the NCTE/IRA Content Standards, NCTE Annual Convention, San Diego, CA, November 1995.

The NCTE/IRA Content Standards, NCTE Annual Convention, San Diego, CA, November 1995.

NCTE AFFILIATE STANDARDS WORKSHOPS

Region 1 (Connecticut, Delaware, Maine, New Hampshire, New Jersey, New York, Rhode Island, Vermont), New Brunswick, NJ, September 10, 1993, and Boston, MA, September 29, 1995.

Region 2 (Kentucky, Maryland, Ohio, Pennsylvania, Virginia, West Virginia, District of Columbia), Baltimore, MD, September 30, 1994

Region 3 (Alabama, Florida, Georgia, Mississippi, North Carolina, South Carolina, Tennessee), Clearwater Beach, FL, January 13, 1995

Region 4 (Illinois, Indiana, Michigan, Minnesota, North Dakota, South Dakota, Wisconsin), Sioux Falls, SD, April 29, 1994

Region 5 (Arkansas, Iowa, Kansas, Missouri, Nebraska, Oklahoma), Oklahoma City, OK, March 4, 1994

Region 6 (Louisiana, New Mexico, Texas), Dallas, TX, September 16, 1994

Region 7 (Alaska, Idaho, Montana, Oregon, Washington, Wyoming, Alberta, British Columbia, Saskatchewan), Vancouver, BC, November 5, 1993, and Missoula, MT, September 8, 1995

Region 8 (Arizona, California, Colorado, Hawaii, Nevada, Utah, Philippines), Phoenix, AZ, February 24, 1995

MEETINGS WITH COUNCIL OF CHIEF STATE SCHOOL OFFICERS (CCSSO)

Conference on Standards-Focused Collaboration to Improve Teaching and Learning. Sponsored by CCSSO, Pew Charitable Trusts, The MacArthur Foundation, and the U.S. Department of Education. Dallas, TX, December 11–12, 1994.

Case Studies in Standards Implementation. Sponsored by CCSSO, Pew Charitable Trusts, and The MacArthur Foundation. Crystal City, VA, December 7–8, 1995.

Draft National Standards for the English Language Arts. Sponsored by CCSSO. Atlanta, GA, October 27, 1995.

Participants:

June Atkins, Montana Office of Public Instruction

Carol Brown, Ohio Department of Education

Miriam T. Chaplin, National Council of Teachers of English

Bernard Floriani, Delaware Department of Public Instruction

Bill Hammond, Georgia State Department of Education

Barbara Kapinus, Council of Chief State School Officers

Janet Langlois, Louisiana Department of Education

Julia MacMillan, Council of Chief State School Officers

Dolores B. Malcolm, International Reading Association

Miles Myers, National Council of Teachers of English

Sharon O'Neal, Texas Education Agency

Angela Rose, Connecticut Department of Education

Joseph Rubin, Fort Worth Independent School District, Texas

Terry S. Salinger, International Reading Association

Helen Schotanus, New Hampshire Department of Education

Kaye Warner, Kentucky Department of Education

Rodney Wilson, Louisiana Department of Education

Donna S. Woods, Oklahoma State Department of Education

Shirley Wright, Longview Independent School District, Texas

Katie Young, Louisiana State Department of Education

MEETINGS WITH THE MODERN LANGUAGE ASSOCIATION

New York, July 1994 and June 1995

Appendix B

HISTORY OF THE STANDARDS PROJECT

The Standards Project for the English Language Arts (SPELA)—co-directed by IRA, NCTE, and the Center for the Study of Reading at the University of Illinois—began work to develop English language arts standards in the summer of 1992. In October 1992 SPELA received a grant from the U.S. Department of Education. Under direction from the SPELA Board, three task forces representing early school, middle school, and high school drafted a framework, standards, and vignettes. Between October 1992 and March 1994, several drafts were circulated to hundreds of review groups in the field for response (see Appendix A for a list of participants). In March 1994, federal funding ceased. Following this decision, the IRA and NCTE boards pledged to continue the work of SPELA, allocating $500,000 each to complete the project.

IRA and NCTE composed and circulated separate standards drafts in the fall of 1994. Joint IRA/NCTE drafts were circulated in the spring and summer of 1995. A final draft was disseminated for review to over 2,500 individuals and groups in October 1995. Throughout the process, IRA and NCTE hosted numerous regional and state meetings on standards and sponsored hundreds of standards-related sessions at their respective conventions. Both organizations worked closely with more than half the states in the development of state standards.

The following chronology highlights key dates in the standards project.

CHRONOLOGY OF THE STANDARDS PROJECT

Summer 1992
- IRA and NCTE boards approve a partnership with the Center for the Study of Reading at the University of Illinois to develop standards for the English language arts. The two boards meet together in the summer of 1992 to chart a course for standards development. The John D. and Catherine T. MacArthur Foundation helps support this meeting in Chicago.

Fall 1992
- Members of the advisory board and task forces are selected.

January 1993
- The kick-off meeting for the Standards Project for English Language Arts (SPELA) is held.

August 1993
- Advisory board and task forces meet; work progresses on standards toward development of *Professional Collection 1*, a "sampler" of the work of the project containing the first draft set of standards, a preamble and introduction, and vignettes.
- Apple Computer, Inc., provides computers for the project.

Fall 1993
- *Professional Collection 1* is distributed for review.
- Advisory board meets.
- Application for continuation of funding is submitted to the U.S. Department of Education (DOE).
- Feedback from reviews is analyzed.
- Jostens Learning Corporation provides computers for the project.

January 1994
- A small group of task force members and staff from IRA, NCTE, and CSR meet to continue work.
- A preliminary face-to-face review with DOE officials is held at the University of Illinois.

March 1994
- The application for continuation of funding is rejected.

Spring 1994
- IRA and NCTE decide to continue the project.

Summer 1994
- Council of Chief State School Officers (CCSSO) expresses interest in becoming involved in the project.
- DOE announces in the *Federal Register* that it intends to publish a request for proposals for the development of standards for English language arts.

Fall 1994
- IRA and NCTE develop separate drafts of standards documents and circulate them to reviewers.
- IRA and NCTE members file objections to DOE's plans to assign English standards to other agencies.
- DOE announces that it will not fund a project to develop standards in English language arts.

February 1995
- Representatives of IRA and NCTE develop a "consensus draft" of standards, which merges the standards that had been developed independently by the two associations.

Spring–Fall 1995
- The work continues as a document is produced and submitted for widespread review and consensus-building.

March 1996
- Standards are published.

Appendix C
OVERVIEW OF STANDARDS PROJECTS

In the past few years, several separate projects have emerged to set standards for the teaching of the English language arts. While many of their goals are complementary, each project has a different focus and a different purpose. This appendix explains these projects.

CONTENT STANDARDS

This book, *Standards for the English Language Arts*, sets forth content standards for the English language arts. Content standards describe what students should know and be able to do in the field of English language arts. The goals of the project have been threefold: to create standards that assure all students the opportunity to develop their unique verbal abilities and to become fully literate citizens in a democratic society; to guarantee access to the most creative and effective English curricula available; and to define a common core of what we value in the teaching and learning of language, emphasizing local involvement in the development of standards.

Articulation of the content standards is a joint project of the International Reading Association and the National Council of Teachers of English (see Appendix B for a more detailed history of the project).

Standards for the English Language Arts is not formally linked to New Standards, the National Board for Professional Teaching Standards, or the National Council for Accreditation of Teacher Education.

ASSESSMENT STANDARDS AND NEW ASSESSMENTS

IRA/NCTE Joint Task Force on Assessment

In 1991, IRA and NCTE collaborated to describe standards for assessment. Their findings were published in 1994 in *Standards for the Assessment of Reading and Writing*. The work of the IRA/NCTE Joint Task Force on Assessment was jointly funded by IRA and NCTE, with additional assistance from the John D. and Catherine T. MacArthur Foundation.

New Standards Assessments

New Standards is developing a new system of assessments (performance tasks, projects, and portfolios) in English language arts, mathematics, science, and applied learning. These assessments are designed to improve the performance of all students and to gauge student progress toward high national education standards. States, districts, and schools will have flexibility to set their own curricula within a common system of student performance standards proposed by New Standards. These performance standards, which are derived from the content standards developed by professional organizations, attempt to specify "how good is good enough." The judges in this process are classroom teachers.

New Standards is a joint program of the Learning Research and Development Center at the University of Pittsburgh and the National Center on Education and the Economy in Rochester, New York. Twenty-one states and school districts are Project Partners; together they enroll about half of the schoolchildren in the United States. The Literacy Unit of New Standards is housed at the National Council of Teachers of English, which holds a subcontract from New Standards. The primary assignment of the Literacy Unit at NCTE is to develop and pilot various models of a portfolio assessment system. Officers of IRA and NCTE have served on the Advisory Board of the New Standards Literacy Unit, reviewing the development of portfolio models.

PROFESSIONAL TEACHING STANDARDS

National Council for Accreditation of Teacher Education

IRA and NCTE are active members of the National Council for Accreditation of Teacher Education (NCATE), which is the national organization for accrediting teacher education programs.

NCATE has approved the guidelines prepared by sixteen specialty organizations as the NCATE standards for teacher preparation in those fields. The NCTE/NCATE teacher education guidelines are those criteria used to evaluate English language arts teacher education programs across the United States. NCATE delegates to NCTE the construction of these guidelines and the actual evaluation of each teacher education program in English language arts which comes under NCATE review. NCTE reviews only the program for initial certification of English language arts teachers, grades 7–12. The review process allows an institution to have its English language arts teacher education program evaluated by a trained team of English language arts educators from across the country.

The National Board for Professional Teaching Standards

The National Board for Professional Teaching Standards (NBPTS) establishes high professional teaching standards and operates a voluntary certification and assessment system. Professional teaching standards specify what accomplished elementary and secondary teachers, including English language arts teachers, should know and be able to do.

NBPTS is a nonprofit organization founded in 1987. The NBPTS Board of Directors is composed of classroom teachers, teaching professionals, other educators, and members of the public. A majority of the members are practicing elementary, middle, and secondary school teachers, and fourteen of sixty-three seats are set aside for leaders of disciplinary organizations.

COURSE AND CLASS CONTENT

The development of standards or curriculum content can take the form of an overall framework, which is the purpose of this document, or can take the form of a course syllabus or a description of one unit or segment of class content. An example of a course syllabus is the Pacesetter course, a challenging capstone English course for high school seniors, developed by NCTE and the College Board and marketed by the College Board.

Examples of class content can be found in the numerous publications of IRA and NCTE which outline standards-consistent content of classes at different grade levels. These publications can be found in Appendix E, which lists teacher resources.

STATE AND INTERNATIONAL
ENGLISH LANGUAGE ARTS STANDARDS

STATE ENGLISH LANGUAGE ARTS STANDARDS

Alabama. (n.d.). *Learning goals and performance objectives.* Contact: J. Steve McAliley, Alabama Department of Education, Gordon Persons Building, 50 North Ripley Street, Montgomery, AL 36130-3901. Phone: 205/242-8059. Fax: 205/242-0482.

Alaska. (1994). *Alaska student performance standards.* An eight-panel brochure. Contact: Judith Entwife, Education Specialist II, Department of Education, 801 West 10th Street, Suite 200, Juneau, AK 99801-1894. Phone: 907/465-8721. Fax: 907/465-3396.

Arizona. (1989). *The language arts essential skills.* Contact: Muriel Rosmann, Writing/Language Arts Specialist, Arizona Department of Education, 1535 West Jefferson, Phoenix, AZ 85007. Phone: 602/542-7840. Fax: 602/542-3620.

Arkansas. (1993). *Arkansas English language arts curriculum framework.* Draft. Contact: David Westmoreland, English Curriculum Specialist, Arkansas Department of Education, State Education Building, Room 107A, 4 Capitol Mall, Little Rock, AR 72201-1071. Phone: 501/682-4556. Fax: 501/682-4886.

California. (1995). *Language arts standards: Draft interim content and performance standards.* Contact: Wendy Harris, Language Arts/Foreign Languages, California Department of Education, 721 Capitol Mall, Third Floor, Sacramento, CA 95814. Phone: 916/657-5409. Fax: 916/657-3391.

Colorado. (1994). *Model content standards for reading, writing, mathematics, science, history, and geography.* Contact: Standards and Assessment Council, C.S. 6, Box 166, 1525 Sherman Street, Denver, CO 80203-9772, *or* Alan Olds, English/Language Arts Senior Consultant, Colorado Department of Education, 201 East Colfax Avenue, Denver, CO 80203. Phone: 303/866-6744. Fax: 303/830-0793.

Connecticut. (1995). *Common core of learning.* Contact: Angela Rose, Connecticut Department of Education, Box 2219, Hartford, CT 06145. Phone: 203/566-4736. Fax: 203/566-5623.

Delaware. (1995). *English language arts content standards.* Draft. Contact: Douglas Grudzina, Department of Public Instruction, The Townsend Building, P.O. Box 1402, Dover, DE 19903-1402. Phone: 302/739-4888. Fax: 302/739-4654.

District of Columbia. (in process). *English language arts/history framework.* A document will be completed in 1996. Contact: Dr. Karin Cordell, Senior Associate, Curriculum Renewal, *or* Gwen Alexander, English Language Arts Content Specialist, District of Columbia Department of Education, 20th and Evarts Streets NE, Washington, DC 20018. Phone: 202/576-7816. Fax: 202/576-7041.

Florida. (1995). *The cornerstone of learning.* Draft. Contact: Susan Watt, K–12 Language Arts Program Specialist, Florida Department of Education, Capitol Building, Suite 444, FEC, Tallahassee, FL 32399. Phone: 904/487-8819. Fax: 904/488-6319.

Georgia. (1991). *English language arts quality: core curriculum.* Contact: Fred Johnson, Coordinator, English Language Arts, Georgia Department of Education, 1954 Twin Towers East, Capitol Square, Atlanta, GA 30334. Phone: 404/656-2586. Fax: 404/651-8582.

Hawaii. (1992). *Essential content.* Contact: Judy A. McCoy, Administrator, Languages Section, General Education Branch, Office of Instructional Services, 189 Lunalilo Home Road, 2nd Floor, Honolulu, HI 96825. Phone: 808/396-2505. Fax: 808/548-5390.

Hawaii. (1993). *Student outcomes for the foundation program.* Contact: Judy A. McCoy, Administrator, Languages Section, General Education Branch, Office of Instructional Services, 189 Lunalilo Home Road, 2nd Floor, Honolulu, HI 96825. Phone: 808/396-2505. Fax: 808/548-5390.

Hawaii. (1994). *Language arts standards of the Hawaii state commission on performance standards.* Final Report. Contact: Judy A. McCoy, Administrator, Languages Section, General Education Branch, Office of Instructional Services, 189 Lunalilo Home Road, 2nd Floor, Honolulu, HI 96825. Phone: 808/396-2505. Fax: 808/548-5390.

Idaho. (1994). *K–12 English language arts content guide and framework.* Contact: Lynette Hill, English/Language Arts Consultant, Idaho Department of Education, P.O. Box 83720, Boise, ID 83720-0027. Phone: 208/334-2113. Fax: 208/334-2228.

Illinois. (1995). *Illinois academic standards project.* Draft. Contact: Lynne Haeffele, Illinois State Board of Education, 100 North First Street, Springfield, IL 62777. Phone: 217/782-5596. Fax: 217/524-1289.

Indiana. (1994). *Essential skills content standards.* Contact: Beverly Reitsma, Language Arts Consultant, Office of Program Development, Center for School Improvement and Performance, Room 229 State House, Indianapolis, IN 46204-2798. Phone: 317/232-9155. Fax: 317/232-9121.

Iowa. Creation and implementation of content standards for all subjects is left to each school district. Contact: Lory Nels Johnson, Language Arts Consultant/Coordinator, Iowa Department of Education, Grimes State Office Building, Bureau of Instructional Services, Des Moines, IA 50319. Phone: 515/281-3145. Fax: 515/242-6025.

Kansas. (1993). *Curricular standards for communications.* Contact: Mel Riggs, English/Language Arts Specialist, Kansas Department of Education, 120 East 10th, Topeka, KS 66612. Phone: 913/296-3379. Fax: 913/296-7933.

Kentucky. (1994). *Content guidelines for writing and reading.* Contact: Kaye Warner, Language Arts Consultant, Kentucky Department of Education, Capitol Plaza Tower, 18th Floor, 500 Mero Street, Frankfort, KY 40601. Phone: 502/564-2106. Fax: 502/564-6470.

Louisiana. (in process). Contact: Katie Young, Program Manager, English, Louisiana Department of Education, P.O. Box 94064, Baton Rouge, LA 70804. Phone: 504/342-0170. Fax: 504/342-4474.

Maine. (1991). *Maine's common core of learning: An investment in Maine's future.* Contact: Wayne L. Mowatt, Commissioner, Maine Department of Education, State House Station #23, Augusta, ME 04333. Phone: 207/287-2550.

Maine. (in process). *State of Maine learning results, English language arts.* Contact: Nancy Andrews, English/Language Arts Coordinator, Maine Department of Education, State House Station #23, Augusta, ME 04333. Phone: 207/287-5939. Fax: 207/287-5927.

Maryland. (n.d.). *English language arts: A Maryland curricular framework.* Contact: Sally Walsh, Division of Instruction, Maryland State Department of Education, 200 West Baltimore Street, Baltimore, MD 21201. Phone: 410/767-0346. Fax: 410/333-2379.

Massachusetts. (1995). *The Massachusetts English language arts curriculum framework: Constructing and conveying meaning.* Draft. Contact: Judith Staten, Instruction & Curriculum Services, Massachusetts Department of Education, 350 Main, Malden, MA 02148. Phone: 617/388-3300 ext. 268. Fax: 617/388-3395.

Michigan. (1995). *Michigan model content standards for curriculum in English language arts.* Contact: Sheila Potter, English Language Arts Specialist, Michigan Department of Education, Box 30008, Lansing, MI 48909. Phone: 517/373-8793. Fax: 517/335-2473.

Minnesota. (1988). *Model learner outcomes for language arts education.* Contact: Al Greenfield, Minnesota Department of Education, 635 Capitol Square Building, 550 Cedar Street, St. Paul, MN 55101. Phone: 612/296-6104. Fax: 612/296-3775.

Mississippi. (1996). *Curriculum structure.* Document to be completed in 1996. Contact: Jeanne Wells Cook, Language Arts Specialist, Mississippi Department of Education, P.O. Box 771, Jackson, MS 39205. Phone: 601/359-3778. Fax: 601/352-7436.

Missouri. (1994). *Communication arts curriculum framework.* Draft. Contact: Charlotte O'Brien, Language Arts Supervisor, Missouri Department of Education, Box 480, Jefferson City, MO 65102. Phone: 314/751-0682. Fax: 314/751-9434.

Montana. (1994). *Framework for aesthetic literacy.* Contact: Jan Cladouhos Hahn, Language Arts Specialist, Montana Department of Education, P.O. Box 202501, Helena, MT 59620-2501. Phone: 406/444-3714. Fax: 406/444-3924.

Nebraska. (in process). Contact: Rex Filmer, English Consultant, Nebraska Department of Education, 301 Centennial Mall South, Box 94987, Lincoln, NE 68509. Phone: 402/471-4336. Fax: 402/471-0117.

Nevada. (1994). *Nevada English language arts framework.* Draft 2. Contact: Julie Gabica, Nevada Department of Education, 400 West King Street, Capitol Complex, Carson City, NV 89710. Phone: 702/687-3136. Fax: 702/687-5660.

New Hampshire. (1994). *English/language arts curriculum framework, K–12.* Draft. Contact: Helen D. Schotanus, Curriculum Supervisor, State Department of Education, 101 Pleasant Street, Concord, NH 03301. Phone: 603/271-3841. Fax: 603/271-1953.

New Jersey. (1995). *New Jersey content standards in language arts/literacy.* Draft. Contact: Roseann Harris, Project Director, New Jersey State Department of Education, 225 West State Street, CN 500, Trenton, NJ 08625. Phone: 609/633-7180. Fax: 609/984-6032.

New Mexico. (in process). *Language arts competency framework.* Contact: Linda Romero, Language Arts Consultant, New Mexico Department of Education, State Education Building, Santa Fe, NM 87501. Phone: 505/827-6569. Fax: 505/827-6694.

New York. (1994). *Curriculum, instruction, and assessment: Preliminary draft framework for English language arts.* Contact: Jacqueline Marino, Associate in English Language Arts, New York State Department of Education, Room 671 EBA Education Department, Albany, NY 12234. Phone: 518/486-7891. Fax: 518/473-4884.

North Carolina. (1992). *Competency-based curriculum teacher handbook, English language arts K–12.* Contact: Michael W. Frye, Subject Area Coordinator, English Language Arts, North Carolina Department of Public Instruction, 301 North Wilmington Street, Education Building, Raleigh, NC 27601-2825. Phone: 919/715-1886. Fax: 919/715-1897.

North Dakota. (1994). *English language arts curriculum frameworks: Standards and benchmarks.* Contact: Clarence A. Bina, Director of Special Projects, Department of Public Instruction, Special Projects Unit, 600 East Boulevard Avenue, 9th Floor, Bismarck, ND 58505-0440. Phone: 701/328-2098. Fax: 701/328-4770.

Ohio. (1992). *Model competency-based language arts program.* Contact: Carol Brown, English/Language Arts Consultant, Ohio Department of Education, 65 South Front Street, Columbus, OH 43266-0308. Phone: 614/466-2761. Fax: 614/752-8148.

Oklahoma. (1993). *Priority academic student skills.* Contact: Claudette Goss, Language Arts Coordinator, State Department of Education, 2500 North Lincoln Boulevard, Oklahoma City, OK 73105-4599. Phone: 405/522-3522. Fax: 405/521-6205.

Oregon. (in process). Contact: English/Language Specialist, Oregon Department of Education, 255 Capitol Street NE, Salem, OR 97310. Phone: 503/378-3602. Fax: 503/373-7968.

Pennsylvania. (1990). *Pennsylvania framework for reading, writing and talking across the curriculum: PCRP II.* Contact: Diane K. Skiffington, English/Language Arts Coordinator, Pennsylvania Department of Education, 333 Market Street, 8th Floor, Harrisburg, PA 17126. Phone: 717/787-5482. Fax: 717/783-3946.

Rhode Island. (1994). *Developing a common core of learning: A report on what we heard.* Draft. Contact: Marie C. DiBiasio, Rhode Island Department of Education, 22 Hayes Street, Providence, RI 02908. Phone: 401/277-2648 *or* 401/277-2649. Fax: 401/277-6033.

South Carolina. (1995). *English language arts framework.* Draft. Contact: Cheryl Sigmon, Language Arts Consultant, South Carolina, Department of Education, 801 Rutledge Building, 1429 Senate, Columbia, SC 29201. Phone: 803/734-8362. Fax: 803/734-8624.

South Dakota. (1996). *Communication standards: English language arts.* Draft 2. Contact: Dr. Margo Heinert, English Language Arts Coordinator, South Dakota Department of Education, 700 Governor's Drive, Pierre, SD 57501. Phone: 605/773-3134. Fax: 605/773-6139.

Tennessee. (1993). *Curriculum framework for language arts: English goals and objectives 9–12.* Contact: Dr. Kathryne H. Pugh, Language Arts/Foreign Language Consultant, Tennessee Department of Education, Eighth Floor, Gateway Plaza, 710 James Robertson Parkway, Nashville, TN 37243-0379. Phone: 615/532-6283. Fax: 615/532-8536.

Texas. (1993). *Essential elements for English language arts.* Contact: Lawrence L. Richard, Assistant Director, English Language Arts and Reading, Division of Curriculum and Textbooks, 1701 North Congress Avenue, Austin, TX 78701-1494. Phone: 512/463-9273. Fax: 512/475-3667.

Utah. (1995). *Standards for Utah, K–6.* Draft. Contact: Richard Harmston, Elementary Language Arts Specialist *or* Mary Beth Clark, Secondary Language Arts Specialist, Utah State Office of Education, 250 East Fifth South, Salt Lake City, UT 84111-3204. Phone: 801/538-7765. Fax: 801/538-7769.

Vermont. (1994). *Vermont's common core framework for curriculum and assessment.* Draft. Contact: Douglas Walker, External Manager, Vermont Department of Education, Teaching and Learning Team, 120 State Street, Montpelier, VT 05620-2501. Phone: 802/828-3111. Fax: 802/828-3140.

Virginia. (1995). *Language arts standards of learning.* Draft. Contact: Kenneth Bradford, Principal Specialist for English/Reading, Virginia Department of Education, P.O. Box 2120, Richmond, VA 23216-2120. Phone: 804/225-2888. Fax: 804/371-0249.

Washington. (1995). *English language arts K–12 curriculum guidelines.* Contact: Gayle Pauley, Reading/Language Arts Supervisor, Washington Department of Education, Old Capitol Building, P.O. Box 47200, Olympia, WA 98504-7200. Phone: 206/753-2858. Fax: 206/753-6754.

West Virginia. (1993). *English language arts instructional goals and objectives.* Contact: Robert Harrison, Director, Office of Professional Development, West Virginia Department of Education, 1900 Kanawha Boulevard East, Charleston, WV 25305-0330. Phone: 304/558-2702. Fax: 304/558-0882.

Wisconsin. (1991). *Guide to curriculum planning in English language arts.* Contact: Ellen Last, Consultant, English/Language Arts Education, Wisconsin Department of Education, 125 South Webster Street, P.O. Box 7841, Madison, WI 53707-7841. Phone: 608/267-9265. Fax: 608/264-9553.

Wyoming. (in process). Contact: Nancy Leinius, Title VI (Chapter 2) Consultant, Wyoming Department of Education, Hathaway Building, 2nd Floor, Cheyenne, WY 82002-0050. Phone: 307/777-6226. Fax: 307/777-6234 *or* 307/777-5421.

INTERNATIONAL ENGLISH LANGUAGE ARTS STANDARDS

Australia. (1994). 1. *A statement on English for Australian schools.* 2. *English—a curriculum profile for Australian schools.* 3. *Using the English profile.* Carlton, Australia: Curriculum Corporation. Prepared by Australian Education Council, the National Council of Ministers of Education. Contact: David Francis, Executive Director, Curriculum Corporation, St. Nicholas Place, 141 Rathdowne St., Carlton Vic 3053, Australia. Phone: 011-613-639-0699. Fax: 011-613-639-1616.

British Columbia. (1992). 1. *Evaluating writing across curriculum: Using the writing reference set to support learning.* 2. *Evaluating writing across curriculum: Student samples for the writing reference set.* Prepared by the Ministry of Education and the Ministry Responsible for Multiculturalism and Human Rights, Examinations Branch. Contact: Becky Matthews, Director, Examinations Branch, Parliament Buildings, Victoria, British Columbia V8V 2M4, Canada. 3. *Primary through graduation curriculum/assessment framework: Humanities strand, language arts English.* Prepared by the Ministry of Education and the Ministry Responsible for Multiculturalism and Human

Rights, Curriculum Development Branch. Contact: Robin Syme, Director, Curriculum Development Branch, Room 206, 633 Courtney Street, Victoria, British Columbia V8V 2M4, Canada. Phone: 604/356-2317. Fax: 604/356-2316.

England and Wales. (1995). *English in the national curriculum.* London: HMSO. Prepared by Department for Education, Welsh Office. Contact: Department of Education, Sanctuary Buildings, Great Smith Street, London SW1P 3BT, England, *or* Welsh Office Education Department, Phase 2, Government Buildings, Ty Glas Road, Llanishen, Cardiff CF4 5WE, Wales.

New Zealand. (1994). *English in the New Zealand curriculum.* Wellington, New Zealand. Prepared by the Ministry of Education. Contact: Learning Media Ltd. Box 3293, Wellington, New Zealand.

Nova Scotia. (1994). *English language arts P–12 outcomes.* Prepared by the Nova Scotia Department of Education and Culture. Contact: Ann Blackwood, Department of Education and Culture, Box 578, Halifax, Nova Scotia B3J 2R7, Canada. Phone: 902/424-5430.

Nova Scotia, Newfoundland, New Brunswick, and Prince Edward Island. (1995). *Foundation for the Atlantic Canada English language arts curriculum.* Validation draft. Prepared by the four provinces. Contact: Ann Blackwood, Department of Education and Culture, Box 578, Halifax, Nova Scotia B3J 2R7, Canada. Phone: 902/424-5430.

Ontario. (1995). *Provincial standards, language, grades 1–9.* Field test version. Prepared by the Ontario Ministry of Education and Training. Contact: Mary Lou Sutar-Hynes, Ministry of Education and Training, 16th Floor, Mowat Block, 900 Bay Street, Toronto, Ontario M7A 1L2, Canada. Phone: 416/325-2376.

Saskatchewan. (1989). 1. *Policy for English language arts kindergarten to grade twelve for Saskatchewan schools.* Summary Paper. 2. *English language arts: A curriculum guide for the elementary level.* Contact: Saskatchewan Education, Training and Employment, 2220 College Avenue, Regina, Saskatchewan S4P 3V7, Canada. Phone: 306/787-6030.

Scotland. (1991). *Curriculum and assessment in Scotland, national guidelines: English language 5–14.* Prepared by the Scottish Office Education Department. Contact: The Scottish Office Education Department, New St. Andrew's House, Edinburgh EH1 3SY, Scotland. Fax: 031/244-4785.

Appendix E

RESOURCES FOR TEACHERS

The following teacher resources are available from IRA and NCTE.

STANDARDS-RELATED BOOKS

Standards in Practice Series

This series illustrates how students, teachers, parents, and schools can work together to meet higher literacy achievement standards. Each book offers descriptive vignettes that demonstrate how enlightened thinking about teaching and learning can foster student achievement in the language arts.

Crafton, L. K. (1996). *Standards in practice, grades K–2.* NCTE.
Sierra-Perry, M. (1996). *Standards in practice, grades 3–5.* NCTE.
Smagorinsky, P. (1996). *Standards in practice, grades 9–12.* NCTE.
Wilhelm, J. D. (1996). *Standards in practice, grades 6–8.* NCTE.

Standards Consensus Series

Books in this ongoing series are designed to serve as useful guides for teachers who are striving to align lively, classroom-tested practices with standards. Each book surveys local, state, and national standards to highlight key topics of consensus and then presents the best teaching ideas from prior NCTE publications on those topics.

Motivating writing in middle school. (1996). NCTE.
Teaching literature in high school: The novel. (1995). NCTE.
Teaching literature in middle school: Fiction. (1996). NCTE.
Teaching the writing process in high school. (1995). NCTE.

IRA/NCTE Joint Task Force on Assessment. (1994). *Standards for the assessment of reading and writing.* IRA and NCTE.

This landmark report is the culmination of a joint IRA/NCTE effort to define standards for assessing literacy in ways that further learning rather than distort it. The report offers guidelines for assessment methods that reflect the complex interactions now recognized among teachers, learners, texts, and communities; that ensure fair and equitable treatment of all students; and that foster the critical, reflective literacy our society requires.

IRA Professional Standards and Ethics Committee & Advisory Group to the National Council for Accreditation of Teacher Education Joint Task Force. *Standards for reading professionals.* (1992). IRA.

Designed to assist in the establishment and evaluation of programs of teacher preparation, to guide the individual professional who seeks to assess and develop his or her own qualifications, and to inform public and state agencies as they shape reading instruction now and in the future.

ASSESSMENT

Education Department of South Australia. (1991). *Literacy assessment in practice: Language arts.* Education Department of South Australia. Distributed by NCTE.

Provides a comprehensive framework for defining and organizing all the various aspects of literacy that might need to be considered in literacy assessment. It also offers teachers a range of practical ideas to incorporate into the assessment process. Grades K–7.

Jongsma, E., & Farr, R. (Eds.). (1993). *Literacy assessment.* (Themed issue of the *Journal of Reading,* April 1993). IRA.

This offprint contains seven articles that address issues surrounding the demand for educational reform; the mismatch between testing and curriculum; and the search for standards and the implications for assessment at the middle school level and in secondary, college, and workplace literacy programs.

Ransom, K., Roettger, D. D., & Staplin, P. M. (Project Coordinators). (1995). *Reading assessment in practice*. IRA.

A video-based staff development program designed to help teachers examine issues and practices in performance assessment, identify new opportunities to observe and assess student reading performance, and reflect on their own assessment practices. The program includes one 45-minute video, a viewer's handbook, a book of readings (28 articles from *The Reading Teacher* and the *Journal of Reading*), and one copy each of *Authentic Reading Assessment: Practices and Possibilities* and *Standards for the Assessment of Reading and Writing*.

Valencia, S. W., Hiebert, E. H., & Afflerbach, P. P. (Eds.). (1993). *Authentic reading assessment: Practices and possibilities*. IRA.

This publication presents nine case studies that demonstrate how the challenge of reforming assessment can be met at the school, district, and state or provincial levels. The studies are written by educators actually involved in efforts to create assessments that match instruction and yield an authentic picture of students' literacy development without sacrificing accountability, validity, and reliability of results.

Yancey, K. B. (Ed.). (1992). *Portfolios in the writing classroom: An introduction*. NCTE.

Classroom teachers from various backgrounds reflect upon how using portfolios has shaped their own teaching. They discuss ways to introduce portfolios into the classroom, different models and assessment practices for portfolio projects, and new kinds of collaboration among students and teachers. Grades 7–College.

BUILDING LITERACY COMMUNITIES

Brooke, R., Mirtz, R., & Evans, R. (1994). *Small groups in writing workshops: Invitations to a writer's life*. NCTE.

Drawing on their own and their students' experiences in a variety of response groups, the authors suggest four principles on which writing-intensive classrooms can be designed: time provided for writing, student ownership of the choice of topic and genre, constant and continuous response to writing throughout the creative process, and exposure to many different people's writing. Grades 9–College.

Golub, J. N. (1994). *Activities for an interactive classroom*. NCTE.

Offers stimulating exercises to shift the process of reading and writing from a solitary activity to a group experience. Grades 7–12.

Golub, J., & the NCTE Committee on Classroom Practices. (1988). *Focus on collaborative learning*. Classroom Practices in Teaching English series. NCTE.

The first section of this book provides guidelines for developing these collaborative learning skills. Other sections contain activities for literature study; writing, revising, and editing; and television, music, and scriptwriting. Grades K–College.

Marzano, R. J. (1991). *Cultivating thinking in English and the language arts*. NCTE.

Describes four patterns of thought particularly compatible with English/language arts instruction: (1) contextual thinking, (2) thinking that facilitates the construction of meaning, (3) thinking that enhances knowledge development, and (4) thinking that results in higher-order learning. Marzano maintains that helping students develop these four patterns of thought will require significant shifts in the form and function of English/language arts instruction. Grades 5–12.

Yatvin, J. (1991/1992). *Developing a whole language program for a whole school*. Virginia State Reading Association/IRA.

Succinctly presents a solid, readable description of the principles on which whole language is based and provides thoughtful responses to many concerns raised by teachers who are starting out with whole language.

EMERGENT LITERACY

Adams, M. J., with Stahl, S. A., Osborn, J., & Lehr, F. (Summary Authors). (1990). *Beginning to read: Thinking and learning about print, a summary*. Center for the Study of Reading, University of Illinois.

Drawn from the larger work of the same title, this summary describes important issues in beginning reading and features a comprehensive review of research from the fields of cognitive psychology, developmental psychology, linguistics, computer science, and anthropology, as well as education and reading.

Goodman, Y. M. (Ed.). (1990). *How children construct literacy: Piagetian perspectives*. IRA.

Presents a wealth of information on children's literacy development. Topics examined include the evolution of literacy development, applications of psychogenetic literacy research to literacy education, children's knowledge about literacy development, and the influences of classroom-social settings on the development of literacy.

Morrow, L. M., Burks, S. P., & Rand, M. K. (Eds./Compilers). (1992). *Resources in early literacy development: An annotated bibliography*. IRA.

Identifies a wealth of resources in a concise, accessible volume for teachers, parents, and administrators; includes books, book chapters, pamphlets, journals, journal articles, videos, and other materials.

Reading and young children: A practical guide for child care providers. (1992). IRA.

This 12-minute video provides general, practical information on the importance of making reading a part of every child's day. The video demonstrates techniques for reading aloud, choral reading, using Big Books, and storytelling.

Roskos, K. A., Vukelich, C., Christie, J. F., Enz, B. J., & Neuman, S. B. (1995). *Linking literacy and play*. IRA.

This 12-minute video with facilitator's guide and book of readings provides early childhood teachers with ideas about how to use the natural environment of play to foster literacy development. Four topics are addressed: exploring beliefs about literacy in play, creating literacy-based enriched play environments, understanding adult roles that support literacy, and promoting literacy while preserving play.

Strickland, D. S., & Morrow, L. M. (Eds.). (1989). *Emerging literacy: Young children learn to read and write*. IRA.

Offers practical ideas for day care workers, classroom teachers, and curriculum specialists.

ENGLISH AS A SECOND LANGUAGE

Olivares, R. A. (1993). *Using the newspaper to teach ESL learners*. IRA.

Addresses the use of newspapers as an instructional tool for English as a Second Language (ESL) students and provides practical suggestions based on solid theory. This book emphasizes using newspapers to teach second-language learners basic language skills as well as math, science, and social studies content.

Rigg, P., & Allen, V. G. (Eds.). (1989). *When they don't all speak English: Integrating the ESL student into the regular classroom*. NCTE.

A collection of essays by notable figures in ESL teaching and research who outline principles and techniques for working effectively with language-minority students in the classroom. Grades K–9.

Spangenberg-Urbschat, K., & Pritchard, R. (Eds.). (1994). *Kids come in all languages: Reading instruction for ESL students*. IRA.

Identifies and answers the major questions surrounding reading instruction for ESL students. Includes topics such as creating learning settings that emphasize communicative fluency, implementing authentic, meaning-centered instructional activities, and assessing literacy development. Grades K–8.

FAMILY LITERACY

Hydrick, J. (1996). *Parent's guide to literacy for the 21st century: Pre–K through Grade 5*. NCTE.

Explains key literacy topics and offers concrete suggestions for activities parents can do at home with their children.

Morrow, L. M. (Ed.). (1995). *Family literacy connections in schools and communities*. IRA.

Presents a wide variety of school-based and organization-sponsored programs and initiatives, from which practitioners and researchers will learn how others are responding to the needs of families and will gain insight into how to develop new programs.

Morrow, L. M., Neuman, S. B., Paratore, J. R., & Harrison, C. (Eds.). (1995). *Parents and literacy*. IRA.

This offprint of the combined April 1995 issues of *The Reading Teacher* and the *Journal of Reading* addresses the growing concerns of educators regarding family literacy. Twelve articles, presenting different perspectives on the issues of family literacy, challenge and encourage educators to review current programs, rethink definitions and perceptions, and reformulate projects and practices in order to develop stronger home/school partnerships.

Morrow, L. M., Tracey, D. H., & Maxwell, C. M. (Eds.). (1995). *A survey of family literacy in the United States.* IRA.

Traces the field's historical development and provides an overview of the current state of family literacy in the United States. Includes discussions of more than 100 sources of information about family literacy issues.

Stoll, D. R. (Ed.). (1994). *Magazines for kids and teens.* Educational Press Association of America/IRA.

Includes descriptions of more than 200 magazines from around the world on topics from car racing to learning French to protecting native African wildlife.

INQUIRY

Bosma, B., & Guth, N. D. (1995). *Children's literature in an integrated curriculum: The authentic voice.* Teachers College Press/IRA.

Details success stories from classroom teachers who have integrated language arts, science, social studies, and other content areas by using children's literature as a bridge. Includes accounts of teachers working with at-risk learners and multiaged groups of students.

Freeman, E. B., & Person, D. G. (Eds.). (1992). *Using nonfiction trade books in the elementary classroom: From ants to zeppelins.* NCTE.

Discusses the genre of nonfiction, the link between nonfiction and the elementary curriculum, and the use of nonfiction in the elementary classroom. The collection contains numerous suggestions for classroom activities and features an extensive bibliography. Grades K–6.

Tchudi, S. (Ed.). (1993). *The astonishing curriculum: Integrating science and humanities through language.* NCTE.

This book delves into the possibilities of interdisciplinary learning and integrated curriculum through the structuring and expressive powers of language. The fifteen chapters explore the issues of bridging the gap between the two cultures of science and humanities, demystifying science for learners, teaching students to construct and explain their own knowledge, integrating science and humanities with society, and creating a language base for learning. Grades K–College.

INTEGRATING THE ENGLISH LANGUAGE ARTS

Flurkey, A. D., & Meyer, R. J. (Eds.). (1994). *Under the whole language umbrella: Many cultures, many voices.* NCTE and Whole Language Umbrella.

This collection brings together respected whole language leaders—classroom teachers, theorists, researchers, and teacher educators—to provide a comprehensive view of whole language. Grades K–8.

Gallas, K. (1994). *The languages of learning: How children talk, write, dance, draw, and sing their understanding to the world.* Teachers College Press/IRA.

Offers a fresh approach to understanding how young children communicate their knowledge of the world with a definition of narrative that includes the many types of communication children use to express their thoughts.

Gere, A. R. (Ed.). (1985). *Roots in the sawdust: Writing to learn across the disciplines.* NCTE.

Teacher-authors from a wide variety of disciplines detail how they have successfully used composition exercises to measurably improve their students' comprehension—without creating a grading nightmare for themselves. Grades K–College.

Primary voices K–6: The first-year collection. (1994). NCTE.

In its first year, *Primary Voices K–6* addressed many of the key issues affecting English/language arts education today—inquiry-based instruction and evaluation, theme cycles, writing to learn, and improving teaching and learning. Grades K–6.

Primary voices K–6: The second-year collection. (1995). NCTE.

> This second-year bound volume addresses important English language arts topics like generative curriculum, conflict resolution, children's literature, and talking and learning in the classroom.

Raines, S. C. (Ed.). (1995). *Whole language across the curriculum: Grades 1, 2, 3.* Teachers College Press/IRA.

> Shows primary teachers what it means to be a whole language teacher and how to incorporate the best whole language practices into their own teaching. Provides classroom models for gradually accommodating this theoretical base for instruction called whole language.

Smagorinsky, P. (1991). *Expressions: Multiple intelligences in the English class.* Theory and Research Into Practice series. NCTE.

> Presents evidence supporting recognition of four scales of intelligence—the spatial, musical, bodily-kinesthetic, and interpersonal-intrapersonal—that are not as commonly assessed as are the linguistic and logical-mathematical competencies. The "Practice" section helps teachers develop learning situations that encourage students to exercise these alternative intelligences. Grades 7–12.

Voices from the middle: The first-year collection. (1995). NCTE.

> This collection highlights the ways that middle school teachers can make learning more meaningful, purposeful, and enriching for their students. Topics include responding to literature, building literacy pathways for at-risk students, developing portfolio cultures, and enhancing reading processes.

LANGUAGE

Cullinan, B. E. (Ed.). (1993). *Children's voices: Talk in the classroom.* IRA.

> Presents a collection of essays designed to suggest ways teachers can help children develop their speaking and listening abilities. Activities such as storytelling, creative drama, small-group discussions, and literature circles are used to lead students to talking, listening, learning, and fun in the classroom.

McAlexander, P. J., Dobie, A. B., & Gregg, N. (1992). *Beyond the "SP" label: Improving the spelling of learning disabled and basic writers.* Theory and Research Into Practice series. NCTE.

> This book provides both research and practical activities to help learning disabled and basic writers become better spellers. Grades 7–College.

Noguchi, R. R. (1991). *Grammar and the teaching of writing: Limits and possibilities.* NCTE.

> Noguchi argues that the main reason formal grammar instruction does not help students improve their writing is that teachers have had unrealistic expectations of what grammar can do. He believes that grammar can help students—but only with style, not with content or organization—and he suggests presenting students with a "writer's grammar" that specifically addresses the problems that crop up most often or those that society deems most serious. Grades 7–College.

Robinson, R. (1988). *Unlocking Shakespeare's language: Help for the teacher and student.* Theory and Research Into Practice series. ERIC/RCS and NCTE.

> With the activities in this book, students can come to understand the language of Shakespeare by learning to recognize and translate troublesome words and syntactic patterns. Grades 7–12.

Weaver, C. (1979). *Grammar for teachers: Perspectives and definitions.* NCTE.

> Discusses the nature of language processes and shows some of the ways teachers can put their own knowledge of grammar to use without intimidating or overwhelming students. The book also presents a basic grammar text for teachers that covers all three systematic grammars: traditional, structural, and transformational. Grades K–College.

LINGUISTIC AND CULTURAL DIFFERENCES

Cook, L., & Lodge, H. C. (Eds.). (1995). *Voices in English classrooms: Honoring diversity and change.* Vol. 28, Classroom Practices in Teaching English series. NCTE.

Organized into three language, composition, and literature strands, nineteen essays affirm that "diversity connotes the challenge and reward of providing quality programs and instruction that tap into the experience that students bring to their learning."

Daniels, H. A. (Ed.). (1990). *Not only English: Affirming America's multilingual heritage*. NCTE.

The book is divided into four sections: the first describes the nature, development, and extent of the contemporary English-only movement; the second looks at the potential impact of the proposed federal English Language Amendment; the third analyzes the causes and motivations of language protectionism; and the fourth suggests political and professional responses to the English-only movement. Grades K–College.

Dyson, A. H., & Genishi, C. (Eds.). (1994). *The need for story: Cultural diversity in classroom and community*. NCTE.

Nineteen contributors explore the nature of story—the basic functions it serves, its connections to the diverse sociocultural landscape of our society, and its power in the classroom. Emphasizing the complex relationships among story, ethnicity, and gender, the book includes within its scope stories both oral and written, those authored by children and by teachers, professionally produced or created in the classroom. Grades K–12.

LITERATURE

Anderson, P. M., & Rubano, G. (1991). *Enhancing aesthetic reading and response*. Theory and Research Into Practice series. NCTE.

Aesthetic dimensions of the English curriculum are explored in this TRIP booklet, which draws upon the reader-response theory of Louise Rosenblatt, as well as the research of James Britton, Alan Purves, Lee Galda, Arthur Applebee, and others. Grades 5–12.

Applebee, A. N. (1993). *Literature in the secondary school: Studies of curriculum and instruction in the United States*. NCTE Research Report No. 25. NCTE.

Applebee provides a scholarly appraisal of the literature curriculum at the middle school and secondary levels, based on a series of field studies examining literature instruction in public and private schools. He concludes that the selections chosen for study in American secondary schools are neither as inappropriate as many critics suggest nor as well-chosen as the profession might want them to be. Grades 7–College.

Beach, R. (1993). *A teacher's introduction to reader-response theories*. Vol. 3, Teacher's Introduction series. NCTE.

Provides a comprehensive overview of the wide range of reader-response theories that have revolutionized the fields of literary theory, criticism, and pedagogy. Beach discusses the relationships between reader and text from five theoretical perspectives: textual, experiential, psychological, social, and cultural. Grades 7–College.

Cullinan, B. E. (Ed.). (1992). *Invitation to read: More children's literature in the reading program*. IRA.

Discusses ways to use children's literature in the classroom with many creative ideas for using poetry, fiction, and nonfiction in a literature-based reading program and for learning across the curriculum.

Cullinan, B. E. (Ed.). (1993). *Fact and fiction: Literature across the curriculum*. IRA.

Discusses how to use trade books across the curriculum in innovative ways. Historical fiction, books from and about other cultures, and nonfiction on a range of topics can enliven social studies units. Favorite books have great potential for teaching common mathematical concepts such as time, classification, and money.

Davis, J. E., & Salomone, R. E. (Eds.). (1993). *Teaching Shakespeare today: Practical approaches and productive strategies*. NCTE.

The first section of the book is a general collection of different approaches to Shakespeare, both critical and pedagogical. The second section focuses on performance-oriented teaching strategies. Pedagogical strategies for using extratextual resources—mostly film, but also live theater, festivals, computerized hypertext, and knowledge bases—are discussed in the third section. Grades 7–College.

Goebel, B. A., & Hall, J. C. (Eds.). (1995). *Teaching a "new canon"? Students, teachers, and texts in the college literature classroom*. NCTE.

Focuses on identifying a practical pedagogy that will serve a dynamic student population and rapidly changing reading lists. Contributors evaluate the adaptability of portfolios, team teaching, theme-based units, alternative assessments, and writing assignments as potential strategies to be employed in "dealing with difference" in the literature classroom. Grades 9–College.

Kahn, E. A., Walter, C. C., & Johannessen, L. R. (1984). *Writing about literature.* Theory and Research Into Practice series. ERIC/RCS and NCTE.

Presents a set of sequences designed to teach students to support an interpretation, explicate an implied relationship, and analyze an author's generalizations. Grades 7–College.

Langer, J. A. (1995). *Envisioning literature: Literary understanding and literature instruction.* Teachers College Press/IRA.

Langer proposes new ways of thinking about literature instruction and its contribution to students' learning. She focuses her theory of literature instruction on creating "literate communities" in the classroom and developing a reader-based pedagogy for all students. The book is rich with narratives of actual classroom experiences in elementary, middle, and high schools in urban and suburban communities.

Langer, J. A. (Ed.). (1992). *Literature instruction: A focus on student response.* NCTE.

This collection of essays by major researchers in the teaching of literature summarizes current classroom practice and reader-response theory and offers practical strategies for instruction designed to engage students creatively in the experience of literature. Grades K–College.

Lee, C. D. (1993). *Signifying as a scaffold for literary interpretation: The pedagogical implications of an African American discourse genre.* NCTE Research Report No. 26. NCTE.

Argues for an instructional model that brings "community-based prior knowledge" to the forefront of the classroom. Students in Lee's urban high school already had an understanding of *signifying,* a mode of discourse in African American speech. In the author's own words, this report provides "an example of an instructional approach which speaks to the problems of literacy in African American and, by extension, other ethnically diverse populations, as well as to the problems that plague literature instruction in U.S. schools." Grades 7–College.

Macon, J. M., Bewell, D., & Vogt, M. E. (1990). *Responses to literature, grades K–8.* IRA.

Provides classroom activities that encourage students to think more as they read and to focus on the literary elements of a story.

Marshall, J. D., Smagorinsky, P., & Smith, M. W. (1994). *The language of interpretation: Patterns of discourse in discussions of literature.* NCTE Research Report No. 27. NCTE.

Drawing on interviews and on the actual language that readers use to interpret and respond to literary texts, the researchers examine the conventions that shape talk about literature in large groups, small groups, and adult book clubs. By looking across contexts, the authors raise challenging questions about the usual ways of talking and thinking about literature and suggest some promising alternatives based on new theories of literary understanding. Grades 7–College.

McClure, A. A., & Kristo, J. V. (Eds.). (1994). *Inviting children's responses to literature: Guides to 57 notable books.* NCTE.

A practical collection of ideas intended to help teachers invite preschool through middle school readers to respond more thoughtfully to books. Each guide's teaching suggestions highlight activities that encourage children to use conversation, writing, reading, and listening to respond to the stories, compare those stories to others they have read, and make connections with their own experiences. Grades K–8.

Meltzer, M. (Ed.). (1994). *Nonfiction for the classroom: Milton Meltzer on writing, history, and social responsibility.* Teachers College Press/IRA.

Advocates enlivening the teaching of history and social studies through the use of well-written trade books; deals both with reading and writing nonfiction and with teaching and learning history.

Nelms, B. F. (Ed.). (1988). *Literature in the classroom: Readers, texts, and context.* NCTE.

Eighteen essays discuss the teaching of literature from first grade through senior high school within a variety of theoretical perspectives.

Oliver, E. I. (1994). *Crossing the mainstream: Multicultural perspectives in teaching literature*. NCTE.

Gives both a rationale and practical resources for providing a more complete treatment of America's literature in high school and college classrooms. Grades 7–College.

Phelan, P. (Ed.). (1990). *Literature and life: Making connections in the classroom*. Vol. 25, Classroom Practices in Teaching English series. NCTE.

Nearly thirty teacher contributors share their classroom-tested approaches and activities for encouraging this response and growth. Part 1 focuses more generally on how students collaborate and create meaning from what they read. In Part 2, the contributors present ways to help students connect with literature through specific reading, listening, and writing strategies. Grades K–College.

Roser, N. L., & Martinez, M. G. (Eds.). (1995). *Book talk and beyond: Children and teachers respond to literature*. IRA.

Details actual classroom dialogues that demonstrate how teachers can achieve the important goal of fostering children's literary development; offers ideas for using children's literature such as forming teacher and student book clubs, teaching and using webbing and language charts, and exploring literature through drama and art.

Rygiel, M. A. (1992). *Shakespeare among schoolchildren: Approaches for the secondary classroom*. NCTE.

Rygiel combines conventional Shakespeare lessons with ideas and teaching practices that address contemporary concerns about teaching this canonical figure to today's students. Grades 7–12.

Short, K. G. (Ed.). (1995). *Research and professional resources in children's literature: Piecing a patchwork quilt*. IRA.

Brings together a volume of research on children's literature that will provide teachers, researchers, and librarians with important information for further research and curriculum development.

Smith, M. W. (1991). *Understanding unreliable narrators: Reading between the lines in the literature classroom*. Theory and Research Into Practice series. NCTE.

Smith takes an honest look at the practice of teaching literature to secondary students. He points to studies that show students learn better when they are actively engaged in drawing inferences from what they read, and underscores the importance of the reader's ability to assess the integrity of an author's characters without relying on either the narrator or the teacher to do the work. Grades 5–12.

Sorensen, M. R., & Lehman, B. A. (Eds.). (1995). *Teaching with children's books: Paths to literature-based instruction*. NCTE.

Twenty-seven essays by teachers, administrators, and teacher educators focus on practical experiences with literature-based instruction and are grouped into eight steps along the pathway to using literature in the classroom: understanding, considering, preparing, modeling, teaching, collaborating, assessing, and supporting. Grades K–8.

Stewig, J., & Sebesta, S. (Eds.). (1989). *Using literature in the elementary classroom* (Rev. ed.). NCTE.

"Many of us were concerned about the fragmentation of reading into several hundred skills. We wondered if reading, like Humpty Dumpty, could ever be put together again." The essays contained in this book provide rationales, explanations, applications, and examples of using children's literature in the classroom. Grades K–6.

Vine, H. A., Jr., & Faust, M. A. (1993). *Situating readers: Students making meaning of literature*. NCTE.

Using an approach they developed and refined over their combined forty-four years of teaching, Vine and Faust encourage literature teachers at the high school and college levels to empower their students as readers—and meaning-makers—of literature. Grades 7–College.

READING

Allington, R. L., & Walmsley, S. A. (Eds.). (1995). *No quick fix: Rethinking literacy programs in America's elementary schools*. Teachers College Press/IRA.

Provides suggestions to improve instruction for all children, particularly those who are at risk and often do not succeed in today's classrooms. Discusses practical matters such as funding, curriculum, and assessment; presents numerous case studies of effective programs; challenges the status quo; and contributes to the work of shaping education for the twenty-first century.

Bishop, R. S. (Ed.). (1994). *Kaleidoscope: A multicultural booklist for grades K–8* (1st ed.). NCTE.

Provides annotations of nearly 400 multicultural books published between 1990 and 1992. To highlight both commonalities and differences among cultures, chapters group books by genre or theme rather than by cultural group. Includes fiction and nonfiction. Grades K–8.

Brailsford, A. (1991). *Paired reading: Positive reading practice.* Northern Alberta Reading Specialists' Council/IRA.

This video-based training package demonstrates the paired reading technique in three different settings. Suggestions for organizing paired reading projects in school or adult literacy settings, samples of inservice handouts, and evaluation materials are presented in the companion guide.

Carlsen, G. R., & Sherrill, A. (1988). *Voices of readers: How we come to love books.* NCTE.

Using more than 1,000 "reading autobiographies" collected over the past thirty years, the authors develop fresh views of reading by listening to the voices of readers who have written about their experiences with books. Grades K–College.

Christenbury, L. (Ed.). (1995). *Books for you: An annotated booklist for senior high students.* NCTE.

Designed to assist students, high school teachers, and librarians, this book surveys more than 1,000 titles grouped by subject into thirty-five thematic chapters. Each entry includes full bibliographic information, a concise summary of the book's contents, and a notation about any awards the book has won. Grades 7–12.

Cramer, E. H., & Castle, M. (Eds.). (1994). *Fostering the love of reading: The affective domain in reading education.* IRA.

Among the questions explored in this volume are: Why do some people who can read simply choose not to, while others read widely for information and pleasure? How important is reading in modern life? What can teachers do to encourage the development of the reading habit?

Duffy, G. G. (Ed.). (1990). *Reading in the middle school* (2nd ed.). IRA.

Combines both theory and practical suggestions for creating effective instructional improvement through collaboration among teachers and university faculty.

Harste, J. C. (1989). *New policy guidelines for reading: Connecting research and practice.* NCTE and ERIC/RCS.

To arrive at the policy guidelines presented in this book, Harste and others at Indiana University reviewed research studies from a ten-year period (1974–84), as well as classroom practices in reading instruction in thirteen states and Canada. The guidelines describe a curriculum in which reading and writing are tools for learning: where children learn to read by reading and to write by writing, and where children are permitted to choose reading materials, activities, and ways to demonstrate their understanding of texts. Grades K–12.

Jensen, J. M., & Roser, N. L. (Eds.). (1993). *Adventuring with books: A booklist for pre-K–grade 6* (10th ed.). NCTE.

Illustrated with photographs featuring the covers of many of the books included, this enlarged tenth edition contains summaries of nearly 1,800 children's books published between 1988 and 1992. Grades K–6.

Kibby, M. W. (1995). *Practical steps for informing literacy instruction: A diagnostic decision-making model.* IRA.

Details steps elementary teachers and special education teachers need to take as they assess a student's reading abilities in order to make decisions about instruction; presents a cognitive organizer of the components and strategies important to a successful reading and a schema for evaluating each student's reading proficiency in a rational and efficient manner.

Mills, H., O'Keefe, T., & Stephens, D. (1992). *Looking closely: Exploring the role of phonics in one whole language classroom.* NCTE.

Through this detailed look at a successful classroom, the authors explain the relationship between whole language and phonics and how phonics, syntax, and semantics work together to help children construct meaning. This book provides practical answers to the questions teachers ask about the role of phonics in a whole language curriculum. Grades 1–6.

Samuels, B. G., & Beers, G. K. (Eds.). (1995). *Your reading: An annotated booklist for middle school and junior high* (1995–96 ed.). NCTE.

Covering young adult literature published in 1993 and 1994, the book contains more than 1,200 annotations organized by topic. Half of the annotations are on nonfiction subjects. Also includes a list of 100 notable young adult books published during the twenty-five years prior to this edition of *Your Reading*. Grades 6–9.

Slaughter, J. P. (1993). *Beyond storybooks: Young children and the shared book experience*. IRA.

A practical, hands-on book for people working with emergent, developing, and at-risk readers in the preschool and early elementary years; inspires creative teachers and children to come up with thousands of projects of their own, and thereby become curriculum planners and developers as they take ownership of their teaching and learning. Includes an annotated bibliography of more than 100 children's books.

Wood, K. D., Lapp, D., & Flood, J. (1992). *Guiding readers through text: A review of study guides*. IRA.

Discusses why and how study guides help students comprehend text, while emphasizing the most effective ways to use these guides in the classroom; gives complete descriptions, along with examples from a wide variety of lessons in primary through secondary grades.

RESEARCH ON TEACHING AND LEARNING

Flood, J., Jensen, J., Lapp, D., & Squire, J. R. (Eds.). (1991). *Handbook of research on teaching the English language arts*. IRA and NCTE.

A comprehensive resource, this book includes contributions from many prominent scholars in English/language arts education.

Harris, T. L., & Hodges, R. E. (Eds.). (1995). *The literacy dictionary: The vocabulary of reading and writing*. IRA.

Drawing on input from hundreds of members of the reading profession and related disciplines, this book defines reading and literacy-related terms along with vocabulary from other areas that contribute to the study of reading. Definitions represent both technical and nontechnical perspectives on vocabulary used in the classroom and in the research arena.

Neuman, S. B., & McCormick, S. (Eds.). (1995). *Single-subject experimental research: Applications for literacy*. IRA.

Describes various single-subject designs in the context of literacy studies; includes suggestions on how these designs can be implemented in classrooms either independently or in combination with elements from traditional statistical analysis or case-study methods.

Patterson, L., Santa, C. M., Short, K. G., & Smith, K. (Eds.). (1993). *Teachers are researchers: Reflection and action*. IRA.

More than twenty chapters explore teachers' reflections on what is really happening in their classrooms. Teacher researchers tackle tough questions and reveal valuable information about both their teaching practice and the research process.

Pinnell, G. S., & Matlin, M. L. (Eds.). (1989). *Teachers and research: Language learning in the classroom*. IRA.

Mixes theory and personal accounts that show how research about children's language learning can be translated into classroom practice. Acknowledged authorities stress the importance of teachers and researchers working together to help children learn language.

Purves, A. C. (Ed.).with Papa, L., & Jordon, S. (1994). *Encyclopedia of English studies and language arts: A project of the National Council of Teachers of English*. New York: Scholastic.

A two-volume overview of English language arts and its teaching, created by NCTE, the NCTE Fund, and Scholastic, Inc. Individual entries provide an extended definition and description of the topic, place it historically in the field of English studies and English language arts teaching, discuss controversies or policy decisions surrounding the topic, and include references to related articles.

Ruddell, R. B., Ruddell, M. R., & Singer, H. (Eds.). (1994). *Theoretical models and processes of reading* (4th ed.). IRA.

Includes four sections: historical changes in reading; processes of reading and literacy; models of reading and literacy processes; and new paradigms. Includes new, revised, and classic models from some of the most prominent members of the profession.

Samuels, S. J., & Farstrup, A. E. (Eds.). (1992). *What research has to say about reading instruction* (2nd ed.). IRA.

Balances theory and practice while reflecting current research and changes in the way reading is being taught.

Shanahan, T. (Ed.). (1994). *Teachers thinking, teachers knowing: Reflections on literacy and language education.* NCRE and NCTE.

Thirteen essays by university scholars and teacher-researchers explore what teachers of the English language arts must know to be effective and how such knowledge can best be assessed.

Simmons, J. S. (Ed.). (1994). *Censorship: A threat to reading, learning, thinking.* IRA.

Examines important censorship cases and explains how they affect teaching and learning. Included are documented accounts of recent complaints and challenges illustrating how censorship undermines the goals of elementary and secondary education and plagues all areas of the curriculum.

Weintraub, S. (Ed.). (1995). *Annual summary of investigations relating to reading.* IRA.

Summaries of research published in periodicals, books, conference proceedings, and other publications related to the field of reading for the period July 1, 1993 to June 30, 1994. Annotations describe qualitative and quantitative research under the major categories of teacher preparation and practice, sociology of reading, physiology and psychology of reading, the teaching of reading, and reading of atypical learners. Includes an author index and a listing of the journals monitored for the summary.

SPEAKING AND LISTENING

Horowitz, R. (Ed.). (1994). *Classroom talk about text.* Themed issue of the *Journal of Reading,* April 1994. IRA.

This offprint contains seven articles designed to help teachers and researchers better understand the possibilities for classroom talk about texts. The articles identify new forms and functions that classroom talk can take as teenagers attempt to interpret or produce texts in school and thereby learn about themselves and the world.

Hynds, S., & Rubin, D. L. (Eds.). (1990). *Perspectives on talk and learning.* Vol. 3, NCTE Forum series. NCTE.

Seeks to render talk more visible and therefore more subject to reflective teaching. Chapters deal specifically with issues such as the role of talk in learning to write; teacher-student talk, the collaborative conference; language diversity and learning; and bilingual-ESL learners talking in the English classroom. Grades K–College.

Trousdale, A. M., Woestehoff, S. A., & Schwartz, M. (Eds.). (1994). *Give a listen: Stories of storytelling in school.* NCTE.

What exactly is "storytelling"—ancient art or everyday conversation, teaching tool or survival technique? In this collection, teachers from elementary through university levels tell tales of rediscovering the power of oral storytelling for themselves and their classrooms. Grades K–College.

TECHNOLOGY AND MEDIA

Costanzo, W. C. (1992). *Reading the movies: Twelve great films on video and how to teach them.* NCTE.

Arguing that films can be "read" as thoroughly as books, Costanzo urges teachers to help students approach films with the knowledge that they are prepared texts, designed and orchestrated to create effects, raise issues, and evoke responses. The book provides an overview of the film genre and illustrates how traditional textual analysis can be extended to cinematic concepts. Grades 9–College.

Fox, R. F. (Ed.). (1994). *Images in language, media, and mind.* NCTE.

In essays examining politics, television, teaching, learning, advertising, war, and sexuality, contributors to this book show how we use images and how images use us. Teachers at all levels will find classroom implications and specific teaching strategies. Grades 7–College.

Garrett, S. D., Frey, J., Wildasin, M., & Hobbs, R. (1995). *Messages and meaning: A guide to understanding media.* IRA.

Presents activities to help students become informed consumers of media messages; specific lessons involving print and electronic media will show students how to access, analyze, evaluate, and produce messages.

Garrett, S. D., McCallum, S., & Yoder, M. E. (1996). *Mastering the message*. IRA.

> Focuses on media literacy as a companion piece to the 1995 guide, *Messages and Meaning: A Guide to Understanding Media*.

Monroe, R. (1993). *Writing and thinking with computers: A practical and progressive approach*. NCTE.

> Monroe offers a rationale and much practical advice for the use of computers in the English classroom. Although he argues persuasively that computers have a place in the curriculum, Monroe is firm in his belief that technology must serve that curriculum. Grades 7–College.

Wresch, W. (Ed.). (1991). *The English classroom in the computer age: Thirty lesson plans*. NCTE.

> The essays are arranged in three groups for students with varying levels of computer skills and contain suggestions for adaptation to various computer facilities that a school may have. Grades 7–College.

WRITING

Bright, R. (1995). *Writing instruction in the intermediate grades: What is said, what is done, what is understood*. IRA.

> Describes what goes on in two classrooms—one a grade 4/5 class and the other a grade 5/6—where both writing processes and products are emphasized. What teachers say and do, how children respond, what children write, and how teachers' and children's expectations and understandings about writing meet and sometimes diverge are all discussed.

Cullinan, B. E. (Ed.). (1993). *Pen in hand: Children become writers*. IRA.

> Shows the important role writing can play in the classroom; offers ideas and suggestions for making writing time fun. Activities include writing imaginative pieces in response to reading, creating exciting nonfiction reports, learning about the steps in the writing process, polishing mechanics, and working on pieces for portfolios.

Dunning, S., & Stafford, W. (1992). *Getting the knack: 20 poetry writing exercises 20*. NCTE.

> Dunning and Stafford, both widely known poets and educators, offer twenty exercises, each covering a different kind or phase of poetry writing. Through this sequence of writing assignments, teachers can guide students toward full participation in and appreciation of the power of poetry. Grades 6–12.

Emig, J. (1971). *The composing processes of twelfth graders*. NCTE Research Report No. 13. NCTE.

> Reports on a case study in which eight twelfth graders were asked to give autobiographies of their writing experiences and compose aloud in the presence of the investigator. Based on her findings, the author suggests changes in the ways composition is taught and the way teachers are trained to teach it. Grades K–College.

Gill, K. (Ed.), & the Committee on Classroom Practices. (1993). *Process and portfolios in writing instruction*. Vol. 26, Classroom Practices in Teaching English series. NCTE.

> Describes the benefits of using portfolios in assessing student writing and tells how portfolios and a process approach help students to build self-confidence and to develop sensitivity about what constitutes good writing. Throughout the sixteen accounts—drawn from the elementary, secondary, and college levels—these teachers stress the value of student collaboration and the necessity of allowing students to rework and reshape their writing to meet the shifting demands of their own lives. Grades K–College.

Harris, M. (1986). *Teaching one-to-one: The writing conference*. NCTE.

> Covers goals of the one-to-one conference, various aspects of the conference, problems that may crop up, diagnosis of such problems, and strategies for developing students' skills. Grades 9–College.

Johnson, D. M. (1990). *Word weaving: A creative approach to teaching and writing poetry*. NCTE.

> Part 1 focuses on the various roles of the poet, on the essential ingredients of poetry, and on suggestions for the beginning writer. Here the author also discusses open forms versus closed forms, as well as misconceptions about poetry. Part 2 contains suggestions for discussion and writing centering on basic themes of human existence. Grades 7–12.

Proett, P., & Gill, K. (1986). *The writing process in action: A handbook for teachers.* NCTE.

This book provides a myriad of ways to put the writing process into action in the classroom and, more important, in students' lives beyond the limited student-teacher interaction. Chapters address each stage of the writing process, explore the possibilities of writing as discovery, and offer numerous innovative ideas to support students' practice of writing. Grades 5–12.

Tsujimoto, J. I. (1988). *Teaching poetry writing to adolescents.* ERIC/RCS and NCTE.

Poetry can be an outlet for expressing the strong emotions of adolescence. The best examples for students are poems by other students because young people are interested in knowing what their peers are experiencing and feeling. They are also less likely to feel intimidated about using these poems as models for their own poetry. This book offers teaching designs and eighteen different poetry assignments. Grades 7–12.

Appendix F

RESPONSE TO STANDARDS FOR THE ENGLISH LANGUAGE ARTS

Setting and achieving high standards is an ongoing, continually evolving process. The standards presented in this volume will not be complete until they are realized at the local level. Please let us know your reaction to these standards and how the process of setting and achieving standards is progressing in your school district or state.

Please send your comments to:

Terry Salinger, International Reading Association, 800 Barksdale Road, Newark, DE 19714
OR
Karen Smith, National Council of Teachers of English, 1111 W. Kenyon Road, Urbana, IL 61801-1096

Name:_____ Check one: _____group _____individual

This response reflects the perspective of (check all that apply):

_____teacher (level_____) _____parent _____English language arts coordinator _____reading specialist _____principal

_____superintendent _____student _____community/business _____other (Please specify _____)

1. Does this document meet your expectations for how standards should explain what students should know and be able to do in the English language arts?

2. How will this document help you achieve high standards for the English language arts in your school or locality?

3. What do you like about this document?

4. What are your concerns about this document?

5. What revisions would you suggest? (Please cite page numbers.)

(Please make extra copies of this form as needed.)